Resource Activation in Psychotherapy

About the Authors

Christoph Flückiger, PhD, psychotherapist, supervisor, is full professor of clinical psychology and psychological interventions at the University of Kassel, Germany. He is also an instructor for clinical training programs in Switzerland and Germany. His research interests focus on understanding general mechanisms of change with a particular focus on alliance and strength-based methods and how they can be implemented in daily practice. He is former Editor-in-Chief of *Psychotherapy Research* and President Elect of the International Society for Psychotherapy Research (SPR).

Günther Wüsten, PhD, psychotherapist, is professor and program administrator of the training program in psychosocial counseling at the University of Applied Sciences, Olten, Switzerland. He was head of the theater department at the Lübeck Cultural Center, Germany. His research interests include the processes of resource activation and self-regulation, particularly in the analysis of aims in life and motivation. He specializes in the instruction of role play in psychosocial counseling and psychotherapy.

Richard E. Zinbarg, PhD, psychotherapist, is a full professor and former dean of the Department of Psychology of Northwestern University, and in The Family Institute at Northwestern University, Evanston, IL, USA. His research interests focus on understanding the structure and development of anxiety and depression, research methodology, basic measurement theory, and techniques, as well as treatments for anxiety disorders, particularly, generalized anxiety disorder.

Bruce E. Wampold, PhD, ABPP, is professor emeritus of counseling psychology at the University of Wisconsin, Madison, WI, USA. He is certified by the American Board of Professional Psychology, and a recipient of the Distinguished Professional Contributions to Applied Research Award (APA), the Gold Medal Award for Life Achievement in the Application of Psychology (APF), and the Distinguished Research Career Award (SPR). His current work involves understanding psychotherapy from empirical, historical, and anthropological perspectives (see *The Great Psychotherapy: The Research Evidence for What Works in Psychotherapy;* 2nd ed., with Z. Imel).

Resource Activation in Psychotherapy

A Strength-Based Approach

2nd edition

Christoph Flückiger
Günther Wüsten
Richard E. Zinbarg
Bruce E. Wampold

hogrefe

Library of Congress Cataloging in Publication information for the print version of this book is available via the Library of Congress Marc Database under the Library of Congress Control Number 2026933320

Library and Archives Canada Cataloguing in Publication
Title: Resource activation in psychotherapy : a strength-based approach / Christoph Flückiger, Günther Wüsten, Richard E. Zinbarg, Bruce E. Wampold.
Other titles: Ressourcenaktivierung. English
Names: Flückiger, Christoph, 1974- author | Wüsten, Günther, author. | Zinbarg, Richard E., author | Wampold, Bruce E., 1948- author
Description: 2nd edition. | Translation of: Ressourcenaktivierung: ein Manual für Psychotherapie, Coaching und Beratung. | Previous English edition published under title: Resource activation: using clients' own strengths in psychotherapy and counseling. | Includes bibliographical references.
Identifiers: Canadiana (print) 20260126462 | Canadiana (ebook) 20260126470 | ISBN 9780889376496 (softcover) | ISBN 9781616766498 (PDF) | ISBN 9781613346495 (EPUB)
Subjects: LCSH: Psychotherapy. | LCSH: Counseling. | LCSH: Self-confidence. | LCSH: Self-efficacy.
Classification: LCC RC480 .F5813 2026 | DDC 616.89/14—dc23

The present volume is an adaptation of C. Flückiger and G. Wüsten, *Ressourcenaktivierung: Ein Manual für Psychotherapie, Coaching und Beratung* (ISBN 978-3-456-86063-3), © 2021 by Hogrefe AG (www.hogrefe.ch), published under license from Hogrefe AG.

www.hogrefe.com

Publishing Offices
USA: Hogrefe Publishing Corporation, 44 Merrimac St., Newburyport, MA 01950
Phone 978 255 3700; E-mail customersupport@hogrefe.com
EUROPE: Hogrefe Publishing GmbH, Merkelstr. 3, 37085 Göttingen, Germany
Phone +49 551 99950 0, Fax +49 551 99950 111; E-mail publishing@hogrefe.com

Sales & Distribution
USA: Hogrefe Publishing, Casemate Publishers & Book Distribution, 22835 Quicksilver Drive, Dulles, VA 20166
Phone 610 853 9131; E-mail customersupport@hogrefe.com
UK: Hogrefe Ltd, Hogrefe House, Albion Place, Oxford, OX1 1QZ
Phone +44 186 579 7920; E-mail customersupport@hogrefe.co.uk
EUROPE: Hogrefe Publishing, Merkelstr. 3, 37085 Göttingen, Germany
Phone +49 551 99950 0, Fax +49 551 99950 111; E-mail publishing@hogrefe.com

Other Offices
CANADA: Hogrefe Publishing Corporation, 82 Laird Drive, East York, Ontario, M4G 3V1
SWITZERLAND: Hogrefe Publishing, Länggass-Strasse 76, 3012 Bern

Printed and bound in the USA

ISBN 978-0-88937-649-6 (print) • ISBN 978-1-61676-649-8 (PDF) • ISBN 978-1-61334-649-5 (EPUB)
https://doi.org/10.1027/00649-000

Contents

Foreword

For more than two decades, my clinical, research, supervision, teaching, and training work has been guided by a simple yet profoundly unsettling question – one that I first asked not in a therapy room, but during a carjacking incident with two teenagers: *What are you good at?* Having survived that encounter, I was left with an enduring realization. Psychotherapy, for all its sophistication and scientific rigor, has often rested on a largely untested and audacious premise: that sustained attention to symptoms, shortcomings, and deficits will somehow carry our clients to a place of healing, fulfillment, and lasting change. What those young people taught me, in a moment of unexpected clarity, was that our therapeutic probing is often incomplete. While diagnostic formulations may give us, as clinicians, a sense of structure and authority, they do not necessarily grant access to the client's inner psychological landscape – the fertile terrain where strengths can take root, grow, and ultimately help clients contend with their wounds and weeds.

Since then, across psychotherapy settings, educational environments, organizational contexts, and digital platforms, I have repeatedly dared to ask a related question: *What has worked before for you that can be refined and deployed now?* This has never meant minimizing suffering or diluting empathy. On the contrary, it has required walking deliberately into dark and delicate spaces with clients – listening closely to their distress, dysfunction, and despair – while also gently inquiring about their resources. Again and again, emerging from fragile and fragmented narratives, I have witnessed stories of resilience, courage, and hope. These moments have expanded not only our shared therapeutic potential, but have also sustained me as a clinician, offering sparks of vicarious resilience that guard against cynicism.

Importantly, psychotherapy outcome research increasingly suggests that strengths are not merely correlates of improvement, but active contributors to therapeutic change, both for clients and, indirectly, for clinicians. In a large and diverse treatment-seeking sample, specific character strengths – most notably zest, perseverance, and judgment – predicted faster symptom reduction, better overall outcomes, and fewer sessions required, even after controlling for baseline symptom severity (Uliaszek et al., 2022). These findings challenge the assumption that strengths are peripheral or secondary to treatment, instead positioning them as psychological resources that shape engagement, persistence, and recovery. The relevance of this stance became especially evident during the COVID-19 pandemic, a prolonged global stressor marked by uncertainty, isolation, and inequity. In our work examining strengths-based actions during this period, we argued that a narrow focus on fear, risk, and pathology, while necessary, was insufficient for sustaining psychological functioning over time (Rashid & McGrath, 2020). Pragmatic activation of character strengths offered a complementary pathway that supported meaning-making, social connection, and adaptive coping, even under conditions of constraint. For clinicians, attending to these capacities not only broadened clients' psychological bandwidth, but also fostered moments of shared hope and vicarious resilience – an often overlooked buffer against emotional exhaustion and burnout in sustained therapeutic work.

It is precisely this empirically grounded and clinically attuned stance that animates *Resource Activation in Psychotherapy: A Strength-Based Approach* by Christoph Flückiger, Günther Wüsten, Richard E. Zinbarg, and Bruce E. Wampold. This volume does not argue against the careful assessment of symptoms, risks, or impairments. Rather, it insists, quietly but firmly, that psychotherapy is incomplete without systematic attention to psychological resources. What distinguishes this book is not simply its endorsement of strengths, but the precision and clinical realism with which resource activation is translated into everyday practice. A number of features set this book apart in ways that mental health professionals will be unlikely to find assembled elsewhere in a single volume.

First, the book offers true open-anywhere clinical utility. This is not a book that demands to be read sequentially or mastered conceptually before it can be used. Due to its concise volume and formatting, clinicians can turn to virtually any page and find a resource-oriented clinical insight, strategy, or skill that can be applied immediately, often in the very next session. In a professional landscape crowded with manuals that assume extended preparation time or strict protocol adherence, this book functions instead as a clinical companion. It respects the realities of time pressure, cognitive load, and in-session decision-making, recognizing that many of the most consequential therapeutic moments occur spontaneously and must be met with clarity rather than complexity.

Second, resource activation is integrated directly into clinical diagnosis and case conceptualization. Rather than being appended as an intervention phase once symptoms have been addressed, strengths are treated as structurally relevant from the very beginning of clinical work. The book trains clinicians to diagnose resources alongside problems – to notice capacities, values, motivations, abilities, and competencies not as afterthoughts, but as elements that actively shape formulation, hypothesis testing, and therapeutic direction. This shift may appear subtle, but its implications are profound. When resources are part of how we understand the case, they naturally inform what we attend to, how we intervene, and what we expect to change.

Third, the interventions are presented in a very condensed form without oversimplification. Many suggestions are distilled to a single distinction, question, or linguistic shift. I reckon this is a rare and deliberate editorial decision. Rather than overwhelming clinicians with procedural detail, step-by-step scripts, or rigid protocols, the book trusts the reader's foundational competence. It offers precision tools that sharpen clinical attention, timing, and stance, while fully honoring the complexity and uniqueness of each case. In doing so, it reflects a deep respect for clinical judgment and for the irreducibly relational nature of psychotherapy.

Fourth, the book achieves genuine transtheoretical integration without dilution. Resource activation is translated into a language that can be embedded seamlessly within cognitive-behavioral, psychodynamic, systemic, humanistic, and integrative approaches. Importantly, this integration is not achieved through vague generalities or abstract appeals to "common factors." Instead, the book provides concrete guidance on how strengths can be mobilized within existing manuals, guidelines, and therapeutic dialogues. Few texts manage to be truly integrative without becoming conceptually thin; this volume succeeds precisely because it remains grounded in clinical process rather than allegiance to any single school.

Finally, the book emphasizes subtle clinical leverage over technique accumulation. It demonstrates, implicitly and explicitly, that the most complex interventions are not always the most effective. Often, it is the small, well-timed shift in perspective, language, or focus that opens an entirely new therapeutic pathway. This attention to the microprocesses of change reflects a deep alignment with psychotherapy process research and seasoned clinical wisdom. It reminds us that therapeutic impact is frequently found not in novelty, but in nuance.

Taken together, these features make this volume genuinely distinctive. It does not ask clinicians to learn yet another model, adopt a new allegiance, or overhaul their practice. Instead, it sharpens what they already do, by training attention toward psychological resources that are often present, powerful, and overlooked. In doing so, it offers something rare in contemporary psychotherapy literature: depth.

Tayyab Rashid
February 2026
President Elect: International Positive Psychology Association (IPPA)
Faculty Affiliate: Human Flourishing Program, Harvard University, Cambridge, MA, USA
Board Member: Values in Action Institute on Character
Honorary Fellow: Centre for Wellbeing Science, University of Melbourne, Australia

References

Rashid, T., & McGrath, R. E. (2020). Strengths-based actions to enhance wellbeing in the time of COVID-19. *International Journal of Wellbeing, 10*(4), 113–132. https://doi.org/10.5502/ijw.v10i4.1441

Uliaszek, A. A., Rashid, T., & Zarowsky, Z. (2022). The role of signature strengths in treatment outcome. *Journal of Contemporary Psychotherapy, 52*(1), 15–21. https://doi.org/10.1007/s10879-021-09523-6

Preface

The practice of psychotherapy and counseling is dedicated to assisting individuals in leading happier, more productive, and satisfying lives, by helping them relieve the distress that motivated them to seek help. Not surprisingly, throughout the history of psychotherapy, the focus has been on distress remediation: How can a therapist assist the client in addressing the issues that brought them to therapy? This perspective leads to a focus on problems and, in the extreme, to the development and dissemination of particular treatments, to relieve the symptoms of particular disorders. It is not only clinical practice that has focused on symptom reduction – the primary outcome of thousands of clinical trials examining the effectiveness of psychotherapy is symptom reduction.

It is quite easy to be coerced or maybe even seduced into the medicalization of psychotherapy. In most contexts, we are now asked to provide diagnoses (*What disorder is being treated?*) and treatment plans (*How will the treatment address the symptoms of the disorder?*) in order to be reimbursed for services, or simply because it is required at the clinic or agency at which we work in. To receive government funding for psychotherapy research, the research must be in the form of randomized clinical trials that examine treatments for particular disorders. Every clinical scientist, whether funded by the government or not, must submit their clinical trials to a government registry and declare what the primary (i.e., the most important) outcome of the treatment is – universally this outcome is specific to the disorder specific symptoms. Reading the academic journals, we predominantly see treatments for particular disorders – manuscripts on the topic of psychotherapy and counseling that do not investigate the treatment of a disorder have a low probability of being published in prestigious journals. And, of course, there is a push to remove psychological symptoms as quickly as possible, since most payers – whether government, managed care companies, or college administrations – require brief (as brief as possible) treatments for particular disorders.

As a result of the focus on brief treatments for disorders, it is understandable that therapists focus on client problems and the psychological bases of those problems. What is the client doing in his or her life that creates problems? How can I, the therapist, intervene to change destructive patterns? Simply put, immense pressure is exerted to focus on symptom reduction.

It is not surprising then, that we can easily forget that clients bring to therapy an immense array of strengths. Clients often have difficulties in a particular area (e.g., marital relationship) but are successful in others (e.g., their career). Even the most distressed and disadvantaged clients use their strengths to manage their own lives, despite having conditions that would frighten many of us. I am continually struck by the unrecognized courage that clients have, to persevere through truly difficult times. Some of us were trained in programs that emphasized client strengths and focused on client development, but it seems to me that the forces of mental health services across the world are conspiring to work against the use of client strengths in therapy.

The dichotomy between the remediation of symptoms and distress versus health and growth is however false. Activating client resources by emphasizing strengths is not incompatible with distress remediation. As this volume discusses, utilizing client resources is an effective way to increase client well-being, as well as reduce distress. In an important way, treatments that activate the client's own resources, personalize the treatment. Moreover, focusing on strengths in therapy is not incompatible with existing treatments. Scientific evidence indicates that incorporating therapeutic actions that utilize client strengths makes existing treatments more effective.

Resource Activation in Psychotherapy – A Strength-Based Approach provides pragmatic strategies that ought to be used in therapy, to help clients recognize and use their own resources in achieving their goals. Sometimes, therapeutic strategies involve simply changing the way we ask questions, focusing on coping and success, rather than frustration and failures. Other strategies involve more elaborate exercises that assist the client in recognizing and using their existing coping strategies, developing new strategies, and using their strengths in ways they had previously seen as impossible. The questions, strategies, and exercises in this volume are deceptively simple, but often simple changes produce the best outcomes. However, a change of therapist mindset is needed – redirecting ourselves from a focus on symptoms and distress to a focus on client strengths.

Bruce E. Wampold, PhD
University of Wisconsin – Madison

Introduction

Mr. M. has suffered from extreme shyness for many years now. He defines his current state as hopeless, and he has more or less given up thinking that he can learn to cope on his own. His shyness and his tendency toward social withdrawal have led him to losing nearly his entire circle of friends. He's been yearning for a partner for years, but every time he sees an interesting woman, he freezes and can't even speak to her. When that happens, his negative cognitions of being the "most boring" man in the world simply overwhelm him. By the time these thoughts have receded, so has the chance of an encounter. These problems have assumed such a predominant position in Mr. M.'s life that he cannot think of anything else or do the things he enjoys most. Recently however, he mustered the courage to look for professional help.

Mr. M. noticed that his therapist does not simply examine his symptoms, but rather also wants to understand his talents. His therapist, for instance, was very interested in Mr. M.'s job as a teacher and in his popularity with his pupils. Up to that point, Mr. M. had nearly forgotten how many interests he had. This in turn gives Mr. M. the confidence that he is indeed receiving competent help – and the hope that his problems can be solved. With the help of the therapist, he tries to strengthen his innate but dormant talents and build on his strengths and wishes to create new behavioral patterns. After seeing how the detailed work with his therapist helped him make progress, Mr. M. gained the certainty that his state of affairs could be changed, which in turn motivated him to continue on with the therapy, and work on himself and his problems.

All of which is easier said than done! This book is meant for psychologists, psychiatrists, social workers, supervisors, and therapists to illustrate practical starting points for detecting an individual's resources and using them in therapy. It is written in an easy and relaxed style, using everyday language, to enable direct integration into the treatment of clinical populations.

Therapists often find themselves in situations in which they must make quick decisions on how to move forward without necessarily knowing in advance the possible solutions at their disposal. To find their way among these possibilities, they need effective therapeutic strategies to react to the situation at hand. A central role is played by the way they handle the individual resources, capabilities, interests, and motivational readiness of the person seeking help. When trying to understand problems, one runs the risk of relegating a person's resources to the back burner by focusing solely on problematic aspects – which effectively assumes the negative cognitions of the person seeking help and leaves patients in their mindset of negative thoughts (Flückiger et al., 2025). Upon starting therapy, people seeking help often feel hopeless and have given up believing in their own problem-solving resources. It is therefore the therapist's job to reactivate the experience of that person's self-effectiveness. One of the first therapeutic goals of therapists is to recognize the problems as well as the strengths, and the abilities of patients to build on these.

The central therapeutic question is, how can I, as a therapist, integrate the patient's resources directly into therapy, in order to achieve the therapeutic goals worked out, together with the patient. This does not mean excluding a person's problematic aspects; on the contrary, a situation favorable to establishing a stronger resource orientation, will simultaneously make a direct handling of the problems easier (Duckworth et al., 2004; Rashid, 2009).

How to Use This Practice-Based Book

This book is intended for clinicians who want to sensitize and inspire themselves to resource-oriented principles in their daily routine. The book and the individual chapters are designed in such a way that you receive a clinical impulse within 5 minutes, which you can apply directly in your following session, for example.

We predict that you will be able to turn to any page in the book and get a reference to a resource-oriented aspect for an immediate therapeutic implementation. These clues may refer to subtle distinctions in the language used and are primarily intended to encourage clinical reflection in individual cases. The specific principles and methods build on existing, well-established transtheoretical interventions and emphasize the focus on resource-oriented and strength-based aspects of the therapeutic process.

The individual interventions are presented in abbreviated form, and we assume that the underlying basic therapeutic skills are known. Some of the interventions are presented in such a condensed form that they are reduced to very specific resource-oriented aspects. Nonetheless, the condensed suggestions should not prevent you from understanding or appreciating the complexity of the individual case.

Our aim is not that you should change your well-established practice. On the contrary, we assume that the principles presented here will create an awareness and confirmation of therapeutic approaches that are, up to a certain point, commonplace and usual in therapeutic practices. At the same time, we believe that the guidance presented here will raise awareness of resource-oriented and strength-based principles in the therapeutic routine. Resource-oriented perspectives are often simply (or not so simply) forgotten in everyday clinical practice.

This book is structured in three parts.

1) The first part presents central principles in the clinical diagnosis of resources that can be applied in the clarification and interpretation of clinical questionnaires and case conceptualizations.
2) In the second part, various therapeutic strategies are presented for recognizing a person's individual resources and integrating them into the collaborative therapeutic dialogue with the patient. These therapeutic strategies can be used in the framework of existing manuals and guidelines to focus on how to "do things."
3) The third part presents examples of strength-based interventions that provide a suitable framework for addressing patients' individual resources in more detail and using them therapeutically.

Based on the many years of research results from both process research and randomized controlled trials presented in the last section, the most complex interventions do not always have to be the most adequate. On the contrary, it is often the small and subtle, not particularly difficult therapeutic aspects that open up the therapeutic path in a new direction.

We hope that this book will inspire you in your immediate therapeutic practice in the here and now. At the same time, we think that the aspects presented here will also confirm your existing practice. We wish you much enthusiasm and also some playful joy in your future therapeutic explorations!

Further Reading

Flückiger, C., Kolle, C., Schürmann-Vengels, J., Rummer, R., & Allemand, M. (2025). Are psychotherapists' first clinical impressions fundamentally biased? An experimental approach. *Journal of Counseling Psychology, 72*(1), 45–55. https://doi.org/10.1037/cou0000766

Flückiger, C., Munder, T., Del Re, A. C., & Solomonov, N. (2023). Strength-based methods – a narrative review and comparative multilevel meta-analysis of positive interventions in clinical settings. *Psychotherapy Research, 33*(7), 856–872. https://doi.org/10.1080/10503307.2023.2181718

Flückiger, C., Vîslă, A., Wolfer, C., Hilpert, P., Zinbarg, R. E., Lutz, W., Holtforth, M. G., & Allemand, M. (2021). Exploring change in cognitive-behavioral therapy for generalized anxiety disorder: A two-arms ABAB crossed-therapist randomized clinical implementation trial. *Journal of Consulting and Clinical Psychology, 89*(5), 454–468. https://doi.org/10.1037/ccp0000639

Flückiger, C., Forrer, L., Schnider, B., Bättig, I., Bodenmann, G., & Zinbarg, R. E. (2016). A single-blinded, randomized clinical trial of how to implement an evidence-based treatment for generalized anxiety disorder [IMPLEMENT] – Effects of three different strategies of implementation. *EBioMedicine, 3*, 163–171. https://doi.org/10.1016/j.ebiom.2015.11.049

1 Systematic Resource Analysis

Systematic resource analysis serves to complement existing case conceptualizations. Both in professional and private contexts we constantly form hypotheses about our counterparts – the way they behave, what they are thinking, what they care about, what makes them uncomfortable, and of course how they relate to us. We make hypotheses of the other person regarding their actual and past problems, and their coping strategies across areas of life (Grawe, 2006).

Such perceptions can be solely problem-centered, thus, in part, neglecting that person's resources (Flückiger et al., 2024; Scheel et al., 2012).

However, parallel to the diagnosis of *problems*, it is possible to look for *resources* in the various areas of life. People often have problems in certain areas of life and desperately try to solve them without realizing that they possess skills and talents that could be used toward achieving their goals. Figure 1 offers an overview of different areas of psychological functioning concerning both talents

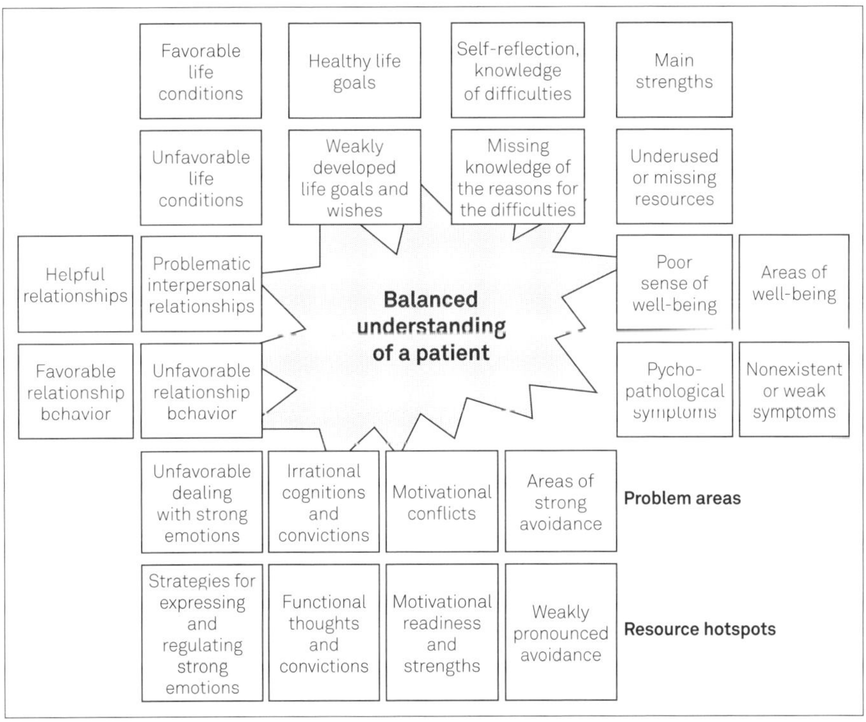

Figure 1. Resource analysis: Problem areas and resource hotspots.

and skills as well as problems and difficulties. Areas with particularly helpful talents and skills we've denoted as "resource hot-spots." One can determine the individual areas through direct questioning or more systematically through professional psychodiagnostics. We do not recommend a particular set of questionnaires because in our experience even the more traditional questionnaires allow one to determine relevant resources, and a useful combination thereof would differ depending on the institutional background. Obtaining an outside assessment from a close third party can sometimes prove extremely beneficial because the person seeking help may be unaware of their own resources (Flückiger et al., 2016, 2021).

Resource hotspots are sources of contentment and well-being. Before therapists develop solutions on their own, they should gain a broad understanding of a person's individual resources. Table 1 lists a few examples of appropriate questions.

Table 1. Possible questions for examining individual resources in different areas of psychological functioning

Individual resources	Sample questions
Favorable life conditions (client and significant other)	What areas in the individual's past and current professional and personal life are considered satisfying?
Healthy life goals	What are the individual's attainable goals, life plans, and wishes?
Self-reflection, knowledge of one's own difficulties	Can the person reflect on his or her own problems? Does the person have a sense of how the problems arose?
Special skills	Does the person have particular skills that stand out from those of others?
Areas of well-being	Does the person have positive memories? In what areas of life has the individual felt comfortable?
Nonexistent or weak symptoms	Where has the complete psychopathological picture not been reached? How pronounced are the symptoms? What caused the situation to worsen?
Weakly pronounced avoidance	Is avoidance behavior limited to certain places, times, or moods?
Motivational readiness and strengths	Does the person show positive motivations such as social integration, connectedness with others, or high productivity?

Table 1. Continued

Individual resources	Sample questions
Functional cognitions and conviction	Do positive thoughts and convictions exist that make it easier to face difficult situations?
Expression and regulation potential for strong emotions	To what extent can the person verbalize and self-regulate emotions?
Favorable relationship behavior	To what extent can the person enter into relationships? What is necessary for this to happen?
Helpful relationships	Does the person have friends and people who can be trusted? Were there any such relationships in the past?

Resource Priming

Resource priming is a systematic way for therapists to prepare by making them focus more on the resources of the person seeking help (see Handout 1 in the Appendix). It helps implement resource analysis in therapy. Figure 2 shows an example of resource priming.

Resource priming is best done at the beginning of a course of therapy in order to flow into the first few sessions. It would be ideal if the therapist were to focus on the resource hotspots and find a way of putting them to good use in the upcoming session. This revisualization of the patient's resources is meant to facilitate the change of perspective (Flückiger et al., 2016, 2021).

Column 1: First of all, the individual resource hotspots that resulted from resource analysis and were explored in the initial conversation are collated. It is important to formulate a workable number of resource hotspots, subsuming individual resource areas in main categories. If in the course of the sessions new additional crucial hotspots are found, these can be documented as well under the heading "Additional resources over the course of the therapy." By collating resource hotspots, the therapist, after a few initial problems, may in the end think of so many different resources that the impression arises that the individual possesses far more resources than the average patient – a first indication in the change of perspective.

Column 2: After identifying the resource hotspots, rank them according to the importance of the patient's crucial needs and motivational readiness. The explicitly motivational meaning of an action is often hard for the observer to recognize, although one can usually assess the importance of the action to the person performing it.

Resource hotspots		How can they be activated?		How well was the resource activated?*				
Test battery/ clinical impression	**I**	**Within the therapy**	**Outside of therapy**	**1**	**2**	**3**	**4**	**5**
Married for 51 years	1	Wife as an expert on the patient's problems and strengths	Mutual activities	4	3	3	2	2
Vivid storyteller	3	Notice, appreciate	Local pub and friends at the camping site	3	3	3	1	3
Self-definition as a foreman	2	Therapy as hard work, tackling things	Personal projects	4	0	0	3	1
Additional resources over the course of the therapy								
Long-time GP	4		Same under-standing of problems			1	0	4
Note. I = Perception of importance for patient/*Perception after the session: 1–5 4 = Extremely, 3 = Very, 2 = Fairly, 2 = Somewhat, 1 = Not at all								

Figure 2. Example of the resource priming of a 72-year-old clinically depressed patient.

Column 3 and *Column 4*: After creating a ranking of important resource hotspots, look for ways to activate the resource hotspots both during sessions and outside of sessions. The goal is to find as many ways of activation as possible. The resource hotspots can be activated independently of the problem areas in question; however, they can also be useful when addressing specific problems. It is vital to document everything, even things taken for granted because otherwise they could be neglected.

Column 5 to *Column 9*: Following the sessions, assess the extent to which the individual resource hotspots were activated in the session.

Further Reading

Flückiger, C., Kolle, C., Schürmann-Vengels, J., Rummer, R., & Allemand, M. (2025). Are psychotherapists' first clinical impressions fundamentally biased? An experimental approach. *Journal of Counseling Psychology, 72*(1), 45–55. https://doi.org/10.1037/cou0000766

Strength-Based Review of Clinical Questionnaires

Psychometric diagnostics of resources may pertain to broad constructs such as well-being, optimism, and resilience, as well as to problem-specific and symptom-specific characteristics, such as the degree of social withdrawal or level of social support. Questionnaires are typically based on constructed Likert scales that measure various stress factors on a bipolar continuum, ranging from a "non-problematic" pole to a "problematic" pole (e.g., "Feeling that most people cannot be trusted?" with a five-point scale: "not at all," "a little," "fairly," "strongly," "very strongly"). When discussing individual results from clinical questionnaires, at least the following four resource-oriented strategies can be incorporated (depicted in Figure 3): (1) validation of stress factors, (2) isolation of stress factors, (3) validation of individual resilience, coping resources and social support, (4) disruption of black-and-white thinking.

1. *Validation of stress factors:* Many individuals seeking psychotherapy have occasionally experienced negative repercussions in everyday life when openly discussing their problematic aspects. Well-intentioned encouragement from external parties can exacerbate feelings of isolation rather than providing hope. Discussing the results of clinical questionnaires offers an excellent opportunity to validate and thus destigmatize the individual stress factors of patients early in the therapeutic process. Patients can usually describe their problematic experiences and behaviors in a detailed, nuanced, and competent manner.
2. *Isolation of stress factors:* Clinical questionnaires generally consist of various (largely independent) dimensions that allow for the localization of individual stressors. Symptom-specific scales are often constructed with a high degree of specificity, making them particularly well-suited for capturing the specificity and intensity of patients' stress patterns, both in problematic and non-problematic directions. This specificity and intensity can be used for situational contrasts (e.g., how could it be worse or better).
3. *Validation of individual resilience, coping resources and social support:* Clinical questionnaires frequently provide an excellent opportunity to explore the potentially non-problematic poles of clinical scales in detail. For general concepts like well-being, the specificity of the scales is often less clear, leading to a tendency for the scales to skew negatively in clinical populations (i.e., lower well-being, self-esteem, hope, gratitude, or kindness). From this perspective, clinical questionnaires are excellently suited for focusing precisely on the non-problematic aspects because they are designed to discriminate effectively between scales.

4. *Disruption of black-and-white thinking:* In addition to validating and isolating problems and strengths, Likert scales offer excellent opportunities for disrupting black-and-white thinking, especially when integrated into comprehensive clinical assessments that consider multiple clinical information

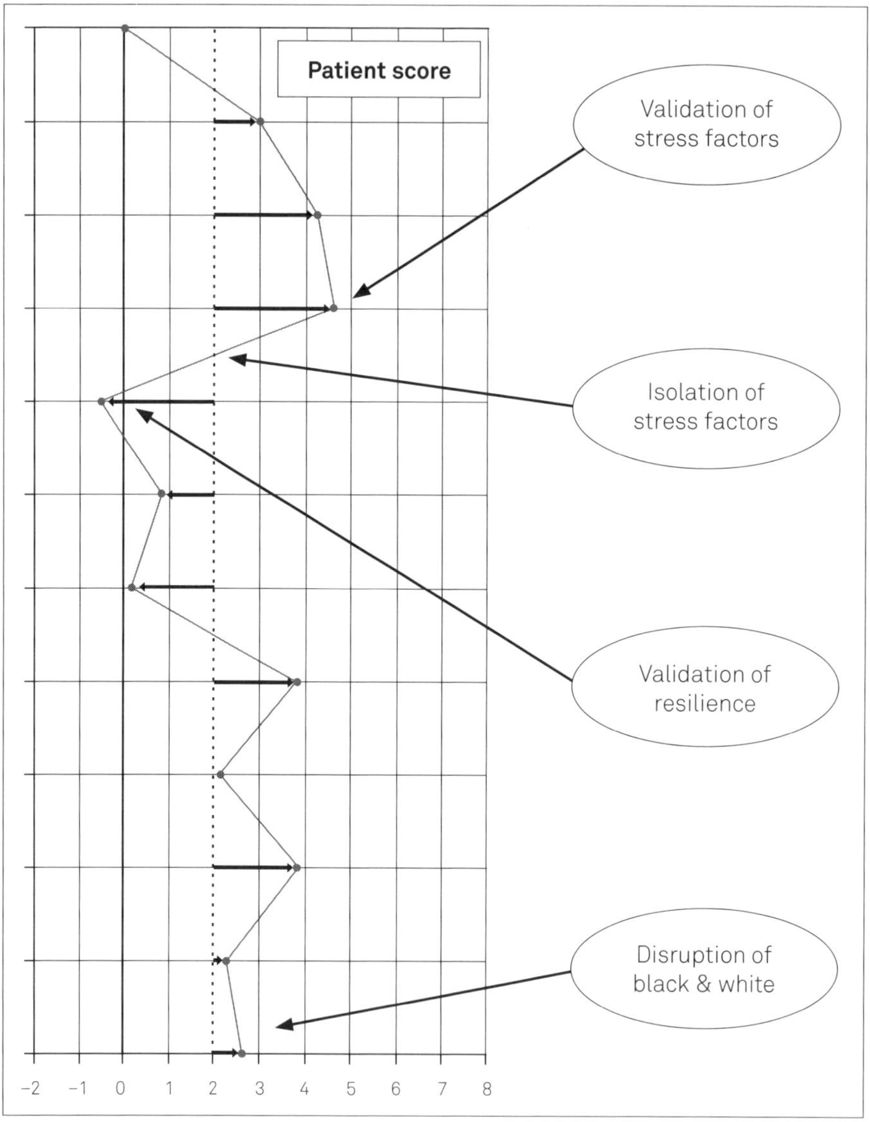

Figure 3. Exploring resilience, coping resources, and social support in clinical questionnaires by setting anchor points (0 = mean of general population, 2 = 95% cut-off point of the general population).

sources. Obtaining an assessment from a close person can provide useful insights, since those seeking help are not always entirely aware of their strengths and resilience (as well as their problems) and may harbor doubts. Therapeutically, the nuanced shades of strength and resilience, as well as possibilities are often significant. Counterfactual thinking can soften unilateral interpretations. Human nature tends to process complex information selectively. During questionnaire discussions, this can lead to an unbalanced co-construction of individual stress and resilience factors. The clinical context generates expectations. Prejudices and social stereotypes toward individuals can significantly influence communication both outside and within clinical settings. For example, patients may tend to self-confirm their negative perceptions of mental disorders (Flückiger et al., 2025; Smith & Grawe, 2003, 2005).

Biases in information processing are insidious in that they are primarily processed subconsciously and do not occur intentionally (Norman & Eva, 2010). One of the most insidious pitfalls in information processing is contrast errors. Individuals often process information in contrast to reference groups (e.g., expectations of the "healthy others' " normal state). This can lead to the perception that problematic states are more problematic than they already are because expectations of others' usual state are overestimated. For instance, as shown by a representative survey by Boehnke and Croudace in England (2016), many individuals might describe their well-being in the last workweek as rather stressful. Yet, in a high-performance society, labeling one's job as stress-free can be frowned upon. However, expectations of others' well-being are generally assumed to be positive (others are happy).

Further Reading

Flückiger, C., Znoj, H., & Vîslă, A. (2016). Detecting information processing bias toward psychopathology: Interpreting Likert scales at intake assessment. *Psychotherapy, 53*(3), 284–290. https://doi.org/10.1037/pst0000081

The Role of Resources of the Patient and the Therapist in Collaborative, Process-Based Therapy

Imagine a career counselor who, during a consultation, systematically reviews all the career fields unavailable to the client, providing detailed and precise explanations as to why the client's apparent deficiencies make them unsuitable for each job. This would likely result in a lengthy, unproductive, and frustrating session. In clinical settings, however, identifying a person's deficiencies and problematic aspects is inherently the goal and purpose of the therapeutic context. Denying or tabooing these problematic aspects would be just as wrong as ignoring a patient's motivational readiness, skills, and talents in diagnosis and therapy.

A resource-oriented approach is fundamentally a general psychological perspective and principle that explores and emphasizes basic psychological concepts such as self-care, social support, psychosocial well-being, healthy development and aging, and intellectual and emotional intelligence within a clinical context. This approach posits that foundational psychological concepts of a "healthy" person in areas like motivational psychology, emotion psychology, social psychology, developmental psychology, personality psychology, biopsychology, neuropsychology, and occupational and organizational psychology are also highly significant when treating patients with mental disorders – not just from a deficit perspective (Scheel, Davis, & Henderson, 2012).

For a nuanced action model, it is therefore crucial to balance the existing deficits and resources on a case-by-case basis. These balancing processes often occur remarkably quickly and subconsciously in everyday life, becoming part of "common sense" and are sometimes hastily dismissed as "trivial" or "obvious." In developmental psychology, Vygotsky's sociocultural model of the zone of proximal development (Cole et al., 1978) describes the difference between a person's current capability – defined by their ability to solve problems independently – and their potential capability, which involves solving problems with the support and guidance of others. The purpose and aim of psychotherapy lie within the zone of proximal development. According to Vygotsky, interventions should focus more on the next possible level of development than on the current state of the person (Cole et al., 1978). From this perspective, therapeutic sensitivity to a patient's untapped or potential possibilities is especially important. If, for instance, the mutually developed goals are set too high, the patient becomes overwhelmed. Conversely, if the goals are set too low, the patient is hindered in their socio-culturally afforded scope of action.

Resource orientation is based on the assumption that therapies, within a social interaction model, are influenced by psychological treatment principles at individual, dyadic-therapeutic, and social levels. Both internal and external factors impact the promotion of mental health, which are significant for shaping the therapy. There is flexibility in designing and individualizing a therapy, which can significantly affect its course beyond the more general framework of a therapy manual (e.g., Wampold & Flückiger, 2023). These design liberties can be utilized more or less carefully and resource-oriented. Resource-oriented levels in the therapeutic process (depicted in Figure 4) between therapist and patient include:

1. *Constitutive Resources*: The individual abilities, skills, and motivational readiness of the patient, the basic therapeutic skills of the therapist, and psychosocial environmental factors which can be systematically considered in therapy planning.
2. *Interactive Resources:* The participants in a treatment jointly negotiate the goals and associated tasks of therapy. Discussions are conducted in a trustworthy setting, with careful handling of therapeutic confidentiality.
3. *Adaptive Resources:* The therapist adapts explanations of the treatment model to the patient's level of comprehension, while the patient assumes a help-seeking social role.
4. *Introspective Resources:* The therapist is aware of their therapeutic abilities and limitations, and the patient proactively seeks their own resolutions.

A major advantage of a broad understanding of resource orientation is that potentially therapy-relevant resources can be comprehensively identified and utilized in therapy. The patient is granted a proactive role in the therapeutic process, which can be used therapeutically.

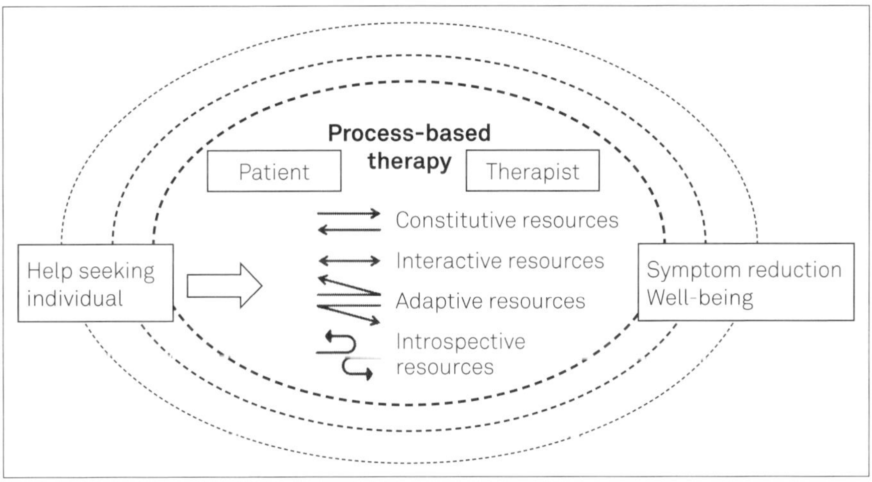

Figure 4. Levels of process-based resources of patients and therapists during sessions.

Further Reading

Scheel, M. J., Davis, C. K., & Henderson, J. D. (2012). Therapist use of client strengths. *The Counseling Psychologist, 41*(3), 392–427. https://doi.org/10.1177/0011000012439427

Wampold, B. E., & Flückiger, C. (2023). The alliance in mental health care: Conceptualization, evidence and clinical applications. *World Psychiatry, 22*(1), 25–41. https://doi.org/10.1002/wps.21035

2 Resource-Oriented Strategies in the Collaborative Dialogue

Manuals or guidelines tend to focus on the description of certain therapeutic interventions – on "what" to do. Often, the "how" is hastily dismissed as obvious and therefore deemed negligible. The following chapter offers an overview of several strategies of resource-oriented dialogue that can be used to channel the individual's attention. Think of it as moving and focusing a source of light or as a resource that can be looked at from various angles. These perspectives are characterized by opposite poles, whereby the two poles of a perspective are in fact complementary.

The job of the therapist is to focus the attention on one or the other pole of a single resource perspective during the session. Patients are often in a state in which they tend to focus on their deficits and are largely unaware of their resources. In order to further an active change of perspective, the therapist has to break out of the patient's thinking patterns.

The goal of resource-oriented dialogue is to heighten the patient's immediate positive emotional experience and thus make it easier for that person to work through problems. Progressive integration of the resource perspective sets a positive feedback mechanism in motion, characterized by an improved working relationship as well as greater openness and cooperation: It reactivates one's own attempts at coping with the problem. In friendly discussions with family or friends, resource-oriented dialogue often occurs spontaneously and is recognized as such only when it is missing. Discussions are then perceived as halting and slow (Grawe, 2004).

It is possible to differentiate between the following perspectives with two opposing poles:

1) Perceiving and validating *directly available resources* and actively searching out *unused resources*.
2) *Verbalizing resources* and immediately *experiencing resources*.
3) Using *potential resources* and integrating *motivational resources*.
4) Strengthening *personal resources* and furthering the *available resources* of the *social network*.
5) Focusing on *problem-independent resources* and taking advantage of *problem-relevant resources*.
6) Optimizing *usable resources* and boosting and maintaining *trainable resources*.

In the following chapters, we explain the individual resource perspectives and point out relevant questions. Short case studies serve to exemplify the change of perspective from a problem-focused one to a resource-oriented one. In contrast, an intervention is always presented in a manner that remains stuck in a problem-focused perspective. We are not suggesting that these questions are not pertinent; rather, we wish to emphasize the technical aspect in the change of perspective. A resource that is not picked up is not necessarily a "wasted opportunity," but can be discussed at a later stage (Flückiger et al., 2023).

Perceiving and Validating Directly Available Resources and Actively Introducing Unused Resources

Perceiving and Validating Directly Available Resources

At first sight it might seem trivial, but recognizing a directly available resource is the result of a complex calculation within a means-ends model in which the therapist has recognized the goals, the potential means of attaining those goals, as well as the function of available resources. Available resources can be so self-evident that the therapist is not even aware of them. Or they might be so "minor" as to prove useful at some later stage and are simply denoted for later use. Additionally, they can be the first small changes and improvements that can then be explored in more detail.

Possible introspective questions for the therapist:

- Have I sufficiently attended to the unproblematic results of the questionnaire?
- Are there any changes or improvements?
- Have I adequately reinforced behavior useful to therapy?
- What is the patient's contribution by coming to the session?

Case Study

Mr. H.: I was jogging this morning, and was not able to get the usual 10 miles. What a shame!

Problem-focused intervention: Do you have quite high expectations of yourself?

Resource-oriented intervention: It seems that you have amazing skills. What makes you so confident about them that they almost seem implicit to you?

Actively Introducing Unused Resources

Unused resources are tools the person has employed in the past but does not actively use any more. Perhaps they have not practiced using these tools in a while or have had some negative experiences in connection with them or can no longer use them to the same extent.

Introducing unused resources requires a careful approach: On the one hand, the solution strategy of the therapist or therapist may be too simple, and on the other hand, the client must have enough faith.

Possible introspective questions for the therapist:

- Does the person have skills they didn't think of in the case in question?
- Does the person have skills they do not feel confident using?
- Were there exceptions in the past?
- Were there exceptions in other areas?
- Has a step been taken in the right direction?

Case Study

Mr. H.: When my wife bosses me around, I just tell myself: "Silence is golden." I do it just to keep the peace.

Problem-focused intervention: So you avoid a confrontation with your wife?

Resource-oriented intervention: Were there any other similar situations in the past in which you reacted differently?

Verbalizing Resources and Immediately Experiencing Resources

Verbalizing Resources

The advantage of talking openly about resources is that the resource can become explicit and consciously applied. It can be assumed that the resource has a motivational background and is thus a source of information for greater motivational goals. Being aware of the exemplary significance of a person's specific resource can give you access to what matters in that person's life and to the tools they use to attain their motivational goals.

Resource-oriented dialogue strategies can happen indirectly, convoluted in subordinate clauses. The therapist can point out what the person is particularly good at, what changes they have gone through, or what they can be proud of

Possible introspective questions for the therapist:

- Can I picture in my mind the resource the person is describing to me?
- Have I understood the subjective significance of the resource for the person?
- What is the influence of the person's "joy" when they tell the story?
- Can I casually suggest a resource along the way?

Case Study

Mr. M.: No really, I like playing soccer in a team!

Problem-focused intervention: That's great! How often did you make the team, then?

Resource-oriented intervention: That's great, and what is it you particularly enjoy?

Immediately Experiencing Resources

By discussing resources in depth, the person may directly experience their resources *in sensu*. Experiencing them immediately does not necessarily mean verbalizing them, however: The ideal scenario would be for the person to find a way of working through them in which they see themselves as particularly competent, for instance, by keeping a tidy diary, precise computer graphics, or efficient notes. In addition, experiencing problem-free areas can be a relief in and of itself.

Possible introspective questions for the therapist:

- What does the patient enjoy and how can I integrate it into the way we are working through the problem?
- How can I adapt the process to the person's skills?
- To what extent can I adapt to the person's own "living space" without giving them the impression that I am pandering (language, metaphors, nonverbal cues)?

Case Study

Mr. K.: It's really hard to fill out this worksheet.

Problem-focused intervention: Yes, I can imagine how that would be a difficult task for you. Still, I think it's important for you to stick with it.

Resource-oriented intervention: Yes, it is really hard. What do you think made you stick with it nevertheless?

Using Potential Resources and Integrating Motivational Resources

Using Potential Resources

Potential resources are existing or unused skills and talents one ascribes to oneself. When potential resources are activated, the person perceives themselves to be active and capable of accomplishing things. Potential resources are the tools employed by the person to achieve their goals.

Possible introspective questions for the therapist:

- What is the person particularly good at?
- What comes natural to them?
- When does the person start to *flow*?

Case Study

Ms. S.: I can barely manage to get through the day, with my little daughter's screaming, my job situation, and an ex who doesn't pay any child support – it's just too much!

Problem-focused intervention: Perhaps you are taking on too much at the moment?

Resource-oriented intervention: It seems to me you are managing a lot of troubles at the moment!

Integrating Motivational Resources

On the one hand, motivational resources are consciously represented goals, wishes, and decisions the person feels committed to; on the other hand, they are motivational schemata and biographically acquired plans used by the person more or less consciously to satisfy basic needs. Motivational resources are, to use an image, the carrots dangling in front of the rabbit that cause him to continue (Caspar, 2024).

Possible introspective questions for the therapist:

- What are the individual's life dreams?
- What idols does the individual have?
- In what areas does the person have positive expectations for change?
- What really matters to the person?

Case Study

D.: I want to be a famous popstar, I don't need to understand math.

Problem-focused intervention: But to be famous, you first have to achieve something.

Resource-oriented intervention: What about when you're famous and you can't trust anyone, then you'll have to do all the math yourself.

Strengthening Personal Resources and Furthering the Available Resources of the Social Network

Strengthening Personal Resources

Personal resources are characteristics, dispositions, traits, skills, and talents used by the individual to satisfy their basic needs. These resources are, on the one hand, personal because the individual can use them at will; on the other hand, the individual feels capable of applying them to attain their goals.

Possible introspective questions for the therapist:

- What makes the person excited?
- What does the person feel committed to?
- What leaves them cold? And why?

Case Study

Mr. M.: If my company goes bankrupt, then I'm responsible for the failure.

Problem-focused intervention: Bankruptcy is dependent on a number of different factors.

Resource-oriented intervention: Free enterprise implies the courage to take risks.

Furthering the Available Resources of the Social Network

People are generally not all-powerful within their social network; they are, however, also not completely at the mercy of that network. Rather, in many areas of life they possess a certain measure of power. Many needs can be satisfied only by being with other people. The social network can include the individual's partner, their family, a best friend, acquaintances from work or leisure activities, a circle of friends or neighborhood acquaintances. Social contexts can be described on many different levels, from individual relationships to one's socioeconomic and cultural context. The breadth of this area should not deter the therapist from looking impartially for all possible resources.

Possible introspective questions for the therapist:

- Is there a strong role model in the family or circle of friends?
- Where can the patient count on social support?
- Is there someone the patient trusts?
- What setting is particularly suited from a resource perspective (individual, couple, family, group)?

Case Study

Mr. G.: I often feel very lonely. Except for one friend, I hardly ever meet up with anybody.

Problem-focused intervention: You often feel lonely and hardly ever meet anyone?

Resource-oriented intervention: What do you and your friend have in common?

Focusing on Problem-Independent Resources and Taking Advantage of Problem-Relevant Resources

Focusing on Problem-Independent Resources

Problem-independent resources are areas in which an individual sees themselves as unproblematic or untouched by problems. These areas can be connected to leisure and encompass favorite pastimes, hobbies, passions, etc. They are also often connected with interpersonal resources. Collecting stamps, for instance, can be an opportunity for (interpersonal) exchange.

Possible introspective questions for the therapist:

- When does the patient see themselves as unproblematic?
- Where does the individual derive pleasure?
- How does the individual find peace and relaxation?
- Were there any good times in the past?
- Did I take the time to allow the patient to rave about their passions?

Case Study

Ms. K.: In the light of my current job situation, my vacation was like being on furlough from prison.

Problem-oriented intervention: What influence did your job situation have on your vacation?

Resource-oriented intervention: What aspects of your vacation had a particularly beneficial effect?

Taking Advantage of Problem-Relevant Resources

Problem-relevant resources are conditions that make it easier to work through problematic aspects. Often the person sees their problems as a bottomless pit or as completely impenetrable. Problem-relevant resources are tied to the problems and define them.

Possible questions:

- To what extent can the problem be delimited in terms of content and time?
- Are there exceptions?
- What caused the situation to change for the better?
- To what extent is the problem understood and to what extent can I validate that?

Case Study

Mr. W.: For me it's like a huge mountain in front of me, and I don't know how to face it.

Problem-oriented intervention: Do you feel stressed out and blocked at the moment?

Resource-oriented intervention: Is it possible that the mountain appears bigger to you than it actually is?

Optimizing Usable Resources and Boosting and Maintaining Trainable Resources

Like problems, resources are not unlimited. The last perspective focuses on maintaining existing resources and preventing a quick-fix attitude.

Optimizing Usable Resources

Material resources are finite, time is precious, and financial resources are exhausted. The resources we use come at a price and can have side effects. And they can be used wastefully or carelessly or not to their full potential.

Possible introspective questions for the therapist:

- Can the quality of a resource be maintained?
- How far can you go before exhausting a resource?
- What are the limits of a usable resource?
- Is the cost-benefit ratio still valid?

Case Study

Ms. T: Since I started working as a flight attendant, with the irregular working hours that it entails, I have been seeing my friends far less.

Problem-oriented intervention: Are you perhaps neglecting your friends?

Resource-oriented intervention: Your friends seem to mean a great deal to you. How can you maintain a good relationship with your friends despite spending less time together?

Boosting and Maintaining Trainable Resources

Trainable resources are talents and skills that have to be practiced and worked at. "Use it or lose it" is true for many areas of cultural and intellectual life as well. Interestingly, trainable resources often act according to the saying: "To those who have, more shall be given." Trainable resources create conditions that maintain existing environments and open up new ones.

Possible introspective questions for the therapist:

- Have I repeated what I have learned enough?
- Is frequency a sensible thing?
- Is there potential for variation?

Case Study

Mr. R: I can afford not to exercise for 6 months because basically I'm a very athletic person. This gives me the chance to study more effectively for my exam.

Problem-oriented intervention: Is it important to you to have enough time to learn for your exam?

Resource-oriented intervention: It seems to me you might be borrowing from Peter to pay Paul.

Resource-Oriented Strategies for Directing Attention

The six resource-oriented strategies (described at the beginning of Chapter 2) function as search-and-find heuristics, allowing the person to generate hypotheses of action and to focus on potential resource-oriented aspects. The heuristics are hence not precise algorithms in a clearly delineated problem-solving space. If all six perspectives are combined together with two poles, we then have a table consisting of 64 squares on which every single resource can be located.

If a therapist encourages a patient with a fear of public speaking to give a talk, an immediate, personal, motivational, problem-relevant, trainable resource is verbalized. However, this division would have little practical use, as a person has many different strengths and the most diverse strengths are often contained in resource hotspots where many things come together. The six strategies are useful for gaining a comprehensive understanding of the psychological function of a person's resources. Thus, it is important to have simple meta-strategies that allow the therapist to maintain an overview of things.

Handout 2 (see Appendix) offers an overview of the six resource-oriented perspectives and the respective introspective questions for the therapist. The aim of these perspectives is to direct attention during the therapy process in the short term. Paying compliments and expressing praise can happen in many ways. Humor can be dry, supported by wild, benign, or vitriolic gestures. It is influenced among other things by cultural values and mores. The dark humor that can help two Scots bond may be hurtful to others. What seems genuine to one person may appear fake to another. Like humor, resource-oriented dialogue is created through the interaction of two interlocutors. It is not dependent solely on the patient, but is rather influenced by the therapist's preferences and fears as well.

For training and self-study purposes, we suggest that you focus first on a single perspective and exhaust it in a counseling and therapy session and then rotate different perspectives. By practicing the perspectives systematically, you will train your perception, i.e., your ability to observe the therapy and counseling process from a specific angle, while at the same time boosting your flexibility, i.e., your ability to take on different perspectives during the entire process.

Resource-Orientation – Strengthening Existing Resources

When building new behavioral patterns, the individual goes through several phases of planning and carrying out the course of action. In general, it is possible to single out four phases (Heckhausen & Heckhausen, 2010; Krebs et al., 2018):

1) In the *choice phase*, different goals are weighed out, and the pros and cons are studied. Eventually, a decision is made in favor of a goal, the Rubicon is crossed and the die is cast.
2) In the *planning phase*, the course of action is planned, decisions are made with regard to their implementation, and the necessary tools are chosen. At the end of this phase a choice is made as to when, where, and how the action will be carried out.
3) The *action phase* follows, the conduct of which is monitored and shielded from external influences. This phase ends with the completion of the action.
4) In the final *evaluation phase*, the action is reviewed and evaluated (see Figure 5).

In order to build new behavioral patterns, these four phases have to be passed through systematically from beginning to end. In that respect it is vital that the therapist not be forced to move to the next phase without giving the preceding phase the complete attention it requires. For instance, an alcoholic might go to rehab without having dealt with the all pros and cons of the changes that might occur. This model has proven extremely beneficial in terms of building new behavioral patterns.

We agree wholeheartedly with this position, but would like also to point out that what is available should be used as would befit the situation. Just as new

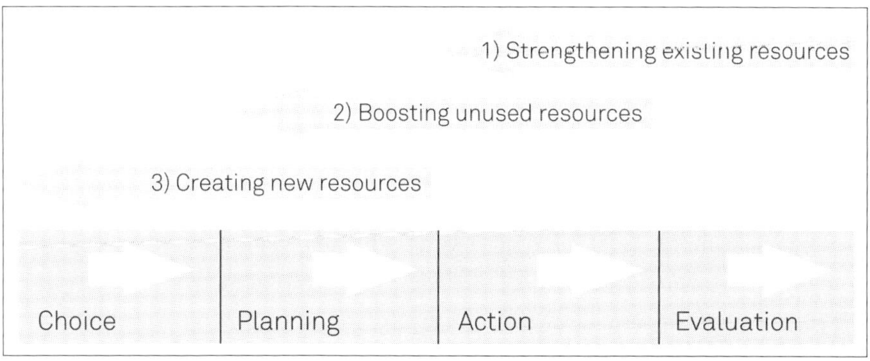

Figure 5. Resource orientation in the general action model.

behavioral patterns have to be built up from the very beginning, existing unproblematic dispositions and decisions have to be used starting from the end point and moving backwards:

1) Existing resources have to be strengthened and maintained.
2) Unused resources have to be boosted and revived.
3) New resources have to be created.

Differences in Self- and Other-Perception

An individual's self- and other-perception do not necessarily agree. What is vital to the therapist is to know the patient's perception from which different interventions can be deduced. If an object is seen by both patient and therapist as a resource, it can also be strengthened and boosted; if the therapist identifies a resource that is not recognized as such by the patient, it is the therapist's duty to introduce the resource *gently*. If it is the therapist who does not agree with the evaluation of the positive resource, he or she should point out the problematic aspects of that resource. And if, finally, something is considered problematic by both sides, its significance and importance can be explored, validated, and potentially defined (see Table 2).

Table 2. Overview of self- and other-perception of resources and the respective task

		Patient/Client	
		Resource	No resource
Therapist	Resource	Strengthening/ mentioning	Introducing
	No resource	Resolving	Validating/defining

Problem Situation and Resource-Oriented Strategies

Resource orientation is dependent on how well the patient has handled the problem. Depending on how aware the patient is of the problem, different resource-oriented interventions will be suitable. As in a means-ends model, three different problem situations and therapeutic strategies can be singled out (see Figure 6):

1) *Problem situation:* Problems are known, goals are unproblematic, and means are clear.
   Therapeutic strategies: It is the therapist's duty to support the patient's intent by maintaining, strengthening, or helping to build potential resources. This happens, for instance, when the therapist points out personal strengths and talents, reinforces positive feelings or interpersonal skills, and emphasizes positive expectations of change, as well as attends to the progress being made.
2) *Problem situation:* Problems are known, but goals and/or means are unclear.
   Therapeutic strategies: It is the therapist's job to strengthen or reinforce the patient's motivational resources. The therapist helps the patient to verbalize goals, to visualize solutions, and to substantiate them – as well as find a balance of goals between means, and finally to come to a decision.
3) *Problem situation:* Problems, goals, and means are unclear.
   Therapeutic strategies: It is the therapist's job to gain an overview of the patient's situation (see Chapter 1) and to narrow down the problems so as to make them appear more manageable to the patient. The therapist can normalize the problems ("You're not alone with your problems"), point to downward comparisons ("How could it get worse?"), work out exceptions ("Are or were there situations when the problem is/was less pronounced?") and reassess problems positively (for reframing, see last section of Chapter 3).

Therapists are often a few steps ahead of their patient without even being aware of it. The inherent danger is that the therapist encourages the patient to take a step before the conditions for it are in place. For instance, they may emphasize

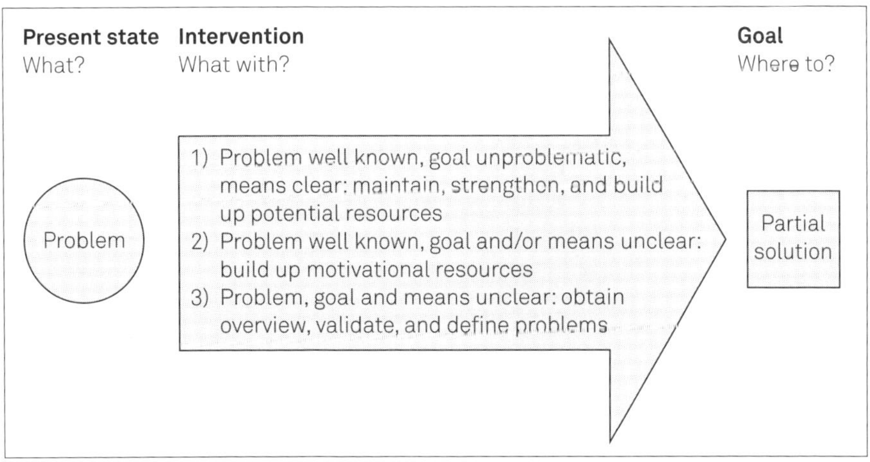

Figure 6. Problem situation and appropriate resource-oriented strategies.

an individual's potential resources for the attainment of their goals (solution strategy 1) before the person knows exactly what goals they would like to achieve (problem situation 2). The therapist has fallen prey to a quick-fix attitude.

Resource-Oriented Strategies Across Treatment Phases

Resource activation as a therapeutic strategy in psychotherapy is based on the strengths and qualities of the individual, which can be used to achieve therapeutic goals. People seeking help often feel hopeless when they start therapy and have often given up believing in their own problem-solving capacities. Revitalizing the person's own coping strategies is therefore a central goal at the beginning of therapy. Resource-oriented strategies have various therapeutic functions depending on the phase of therapy (Howard et al.,1993; Moggia et al., 2020).

Early in therapy (remoralization). Fostering preexisting resources, reactivation of formerly invested resources, and building up of new resources:

- Assessing resources.
- Estimating and validating preexisting strengths.
- Integrating individual strengths into the case formulation.
- Using positive expectations.
- Consolidating therapy motivation and motivation to change.
- Inducing hope.
- Setting up a therapeutic alliance based on strengths and problems.
- Analyzing early gains.
- Promoting self-efficacy and control expectations.
- Isolating patient problems.

Middle of therapy (remediation). Facilitating approach to a problem by making individual resources apparent:

- Reinforcing patient's active participation in therapeutic work.
- Working out a rationale based on individual strengths.
- Using successful coping strategies.
- Using successful problem-solving strategies.
- Choosing (therapeutic) interventions that conform to the patient's preexisting strengths.
- Intensifying problem approach by validating preexisting capabilities and goals.
- Fostering acceptance of unalterable constraints by pointing out existing strengths.

End of therapy (rehabilitation). Consolidation and development of new behaviors:

- Consolidating newly acquired skills.
- Fostering the transfer and extension of these skills to other situations.
- Boosting well-being.
- Maintaining resiliency.
- Fostering self-efficacy, self-esteem, and autonomy.

Risks and Side Effects of Resource-Oriented Strategies

Therapists often voice the fear that too emphatic praise may be perceived as flattery. But this is not necessarily the case. In a study we carried out ourselves, of the 6247 minutes we monitored, trained external observers rated the resource activation as excessive in only 6 minutes – even when the trained therapists were instructed to maximize resource activation (Flückiger et al., 2009; 2013).

The following difficulties could arise:

- Resource analysis is no substitute for a balanced personalized case formulation (Chapter 1).
- Often solutions seem simple and obvious, prompting the therapist to strive to implement them as quickly as possible. Do not! Problems may be misunderstood, and solutions may end up being imposed on the patient (end of Chapter 2).
- Any resource activation coming as an afterthought following a difficult therapy session and beginning with the word "but" may be perceived as appeasement. Resource activation has to be integrated into the therapy and counseling process at an early stage, and then progressively extended – and not tacked on as an afterthought, in an act of self-exoneration.
- Goals can be too ambitious, so that the difference between the state actually experienced, and the desired state, may be too large. This can lead to resistance or frustration.
- Extreme praise for something that is a matter of course can be perceived as patronizing. Example: "It's great of you to always be exactly on time for our session, Mr. Swatch!"
- The therapist tries desperately to build up new resources instead of using existing ones (end of Chapter 2).
- The therapist strengthens problem behavior by not paying enough attention to the problematic aspects of a resource. For instance, assertiveness present in an antisocial person is not automatically a resource (end of Chapter 2).

- "That's easy for you to say! You're a therapist!" Don't let this answer irritate you. Here is a possible response: "Of course I'm a therapist. What is central, however, is how you feel about this."

3 Resource-Activating Interventions

In the following chapter, we describe therapeutic interventions that can engender whole chains of resource activations and structure sessions. Drawing up a life overview can take up a whole session, and even miracle questions, working out goals, or preparing an imagination, require a certain amount of time. As with all interventions, the only sensible ones are those that tie in with the clients' skills and motivational dispositions. For instance, visualization is not right for every person undergoing therapy. Moreover, resource-oriented structural interventions can also be carried out in a problem-focused way. The methods work depends on the specific case conditions and institutional framework. Structural interventions offer particularly good prerequisites for directing the person's attention to their resources and deepening them.

Life Review

In order to create an environment that is simultaneously comfortable and structured, working out a life overview can prove beneficial. The goal is to understand the development of both the client's problems and resources. It is important to find – in collaboration with the patient/client – a coherent explanation for their problems on the basis of their life experiences. And yet, resources must be constantly monitored. Particularly positive life events are stressed from this angle and probed in more depth through relevant questions: "Can you please tell me about this event in more detail? What were you feeling when that was happening? What were others thinking about you? How exactly did you achieve that? How do you feel today having experienced the event?"

Procedure

The initial phase of psychotherapy is fundamentally well-suited to the creation of a life review. A life review contains important events of an individual's life. Life events are recorded on several overlapping timelines, which form thematic focal points. Education/schooling, family life, important relationships, and romantic relationships have proved useful. Depending on the particular situation, additional timelines can be created for specific themes, e.g., travel, health issues, etc. When the timelines are discussed, the therapist should be able to visualize the situation at a specific point in time. Although the topics themselves may seem banal, it is not a matter of asking standard questions; rather, it is vital that the resource perspective dictate the questions. In the case of education and schooling, for example, the questions might be: "What were your favorite subjects?," "Did you have a favorite teacher?," "What did you like about them?," "What did you learn about them?," "What was your relationship with other pupils?," "If you had to define your role, how would you characterize it?"

The therapist tries to find anchor points in the biography which can be coupled with high emotional stages (positive and negative). In the context of the questions mentioned above, difficulties may arise, and problems may come to the forefront. Those difficult experiences should not be suppressed or negated. Yet it is also important not to get stuck in difficult problems, but rather to gain a complete overview, so that both negative and positive events can find their place within the overview. The acknowledged presence of both sides alone can lead to an expansion of the patient's consciousness.

One simple way to ensure this is to make sure the life review starts off with some everyday aspect of life (e.g., education/schooling). Later, the therapist can gain a broader overview of the patient's situation. In addition, the level of discussion can be deepened through the use of "how" questions.

The review can also be recorded on a flip chart, which makes the information readily available to both partners. Over the course of the work, a full picture will emerge, structurally similar to mind mapping.

If the therapist realizes that the person seeking help is happy about specific events in their life, he can delve deeper, by asking, for instance: "How did you feel at the time?", "How did that happen?", "Which people were present?", "Who knows about the event?". The goal of asking such open-ended questions is to keep the patient within the resource space for as long as possible. The life review is hence primarily a form of positive life feedback that can later prove to be a vital resource in the therapy.

Potential Difficulties

Drawing up a life overview generally presents few difficulties. It is important that the therapist take advantage of as many opportunities as possible to activate resources. This can be done by showing interest, paying close attention, being precise, and offering paths to deepening the conversation. The intervention may become problematic when, in the light of extremely difficult life conditions, there are barely any positive events present in the overview, for example, in connection with a clinically depressed state. However, even in such cases, positive events within the different areas (education, family, relationships) can still usually be found and allow for deeper discussion. Central to this context is that the therapist recognizes resources as such and leads the conversation in that direction by showing interest and consistency.

Further Reading

Lin, J., Zhao, R., Li, H., Lei, Y., & Cuijpers, P. (2023). Looking back on life: An updated meta-analysis of the effect of life review therapy and reminiscence on late-life depression. *Journal of Affective Disorders, 347*, 163–174. https://doi.org/10.1016/j.jad.2023.11.050

Genograms and Ecomaps From a Resource Perspective

From a resource perspective, the genogram brings the interpersonal resources from the family's past to the forefront. A genogram usually records family relationships over several generations, including relationships, problematic family events, and fortunes as well as illnesses, births, and deaths. A genogram offers, in compressed form, an overview of all the problematic events from family history and a person's specific biography.

Procedure

In contrast to the procedure usually employed when drawing up genograms, which focuses on problems, here it is the family's resources that are the central aspect (McGoldrick et al., 2020). The perspective covers several generations, going back at least to the grandparents (see Figure 7). This procedure allows for a comprehensive resource search within the family systems together with the patient/client. Over the course of preparing the genogram, the roles and the relationships within the family become clear. Particularly important are the relationships in which the patient felt protected and understood. Individual family members can also become examples for the patient to follow and thus valuable role models. In that respect, perceived attractiveness and closeness to the model as well as the value of the resource play vital roles.
The following questions can serve as central questions:

- Whom were you particularly fond of as a child?
- Which of your mother's/father's skills do you particularly appreciate?
- What positive things have you learned from your father/mother?
- What life skills did your family impart to you?
- What resources did your relatives possess?
- What positive myths or stories are there about your family?
- Is there a family treasure?

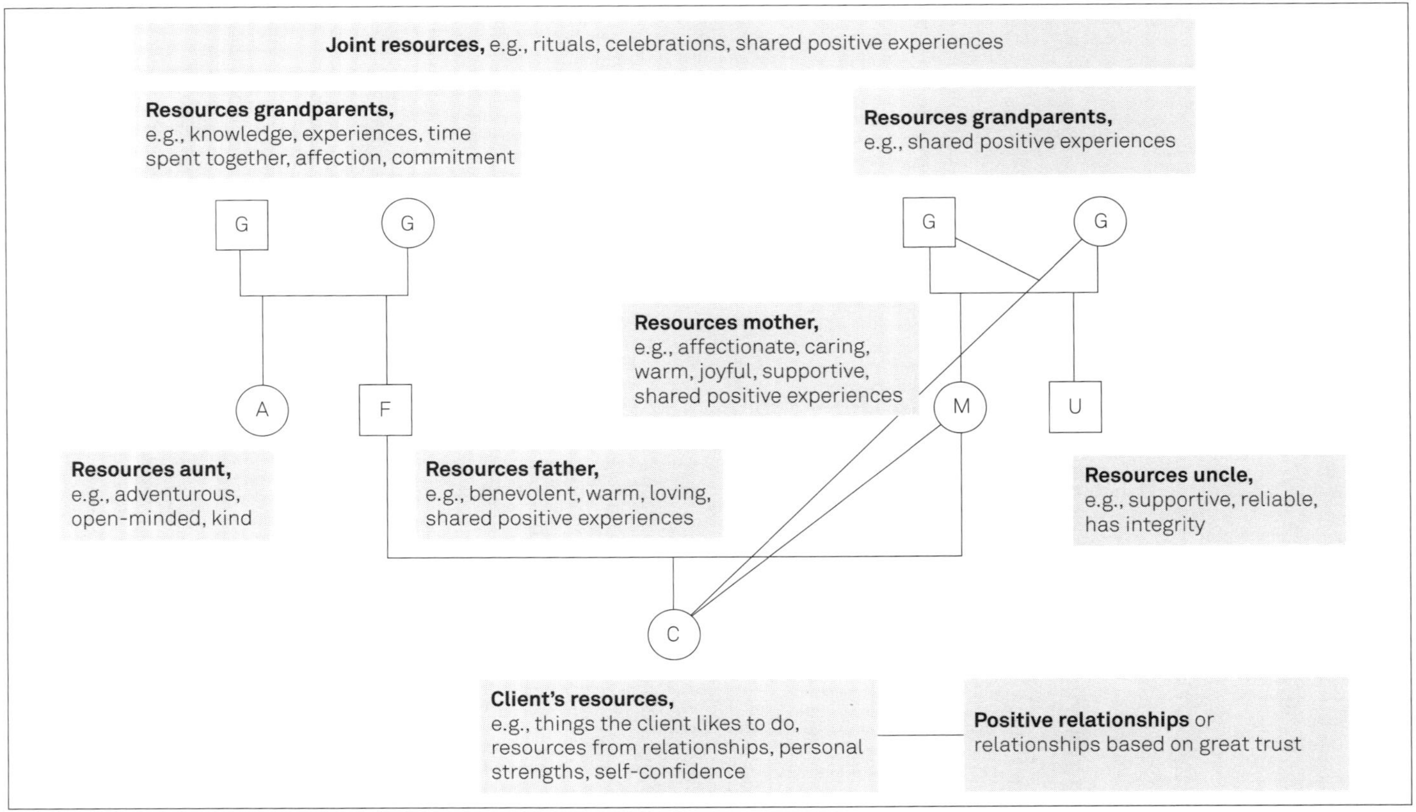

Figure 7. Genogram from a resource perspective. A = aunt, C = client, F = father, G = grandfather/grandmother, M = mother, U = uncle.

An ecogram/ecomap (Hartman, 1995) and social network analysis (Broda et al., 2023), on the other hand, allow us to visualize social connections that reach beyond the immediate family. Social networks and social perspectives are taken into consideration, allowing for further systems to be included in the activation of resources.

Potential Difficulties

Not unlike a genogram, an ecomap consists of highly emotional content. The social links perceived as resources by the client are clearly marked and in addition other network elements that may also have resource potential are recorded on the ecomap. The realization alone that social resources exist inevitably leads to an improvement in the patient's well-being by counteracting the loneliness patients often feel. Unlike a genogram, however, an ecogram represents the family embedded in its environment, the aspect of time is largely left out of the equation because an ecomap usually refers to the present situation (see Figure 8). Potential difficulties in focusing on the family's resources when drawing up a genogram may arise when working with survivors of incest and other forms of abuse within the family. Certainly, with such patients, it is vital to validate their suffering and to not minimize their abuse in any way. At the same time, in later stages of therapy with such patients, after a solid working alliance has already been firmly established, it can be useful to turn to possible strengths, resources, and loved parts of the family and even the abuser after the survivor's suffering has been validated. If nothing else, the very fact that the patient survived the abuse can be framed as revealing internal resources and strength. In addition, even if the survivor is not willing to consider positive aspects of the abuser, in many cases the patient will be able to identify one or more family members with whom they had a generally trusting and caring relationship with, and these relationships can be focused on when focusing on the family's resources. A genogram clearly includes past experiences and emphasizes the patient's personal learning history and family system. Sometimes groups can be a vital resource to the patient, in which case sociograms drawn up from a resource perspective can be used.

Further Reading

McGoldrick, M., Gerson, R., & Petry, S. (2020). *Genograms: Assessment and treatment*. W. W. Norton.

Broda, M. D., Granger, K., Chow, J., & Ross, E. (2023). Using social network analysis in applied psychological research: A tutorial. *Psychological Methods, 28*(4), 791–805. https://doi.org/10.1037/met0000451

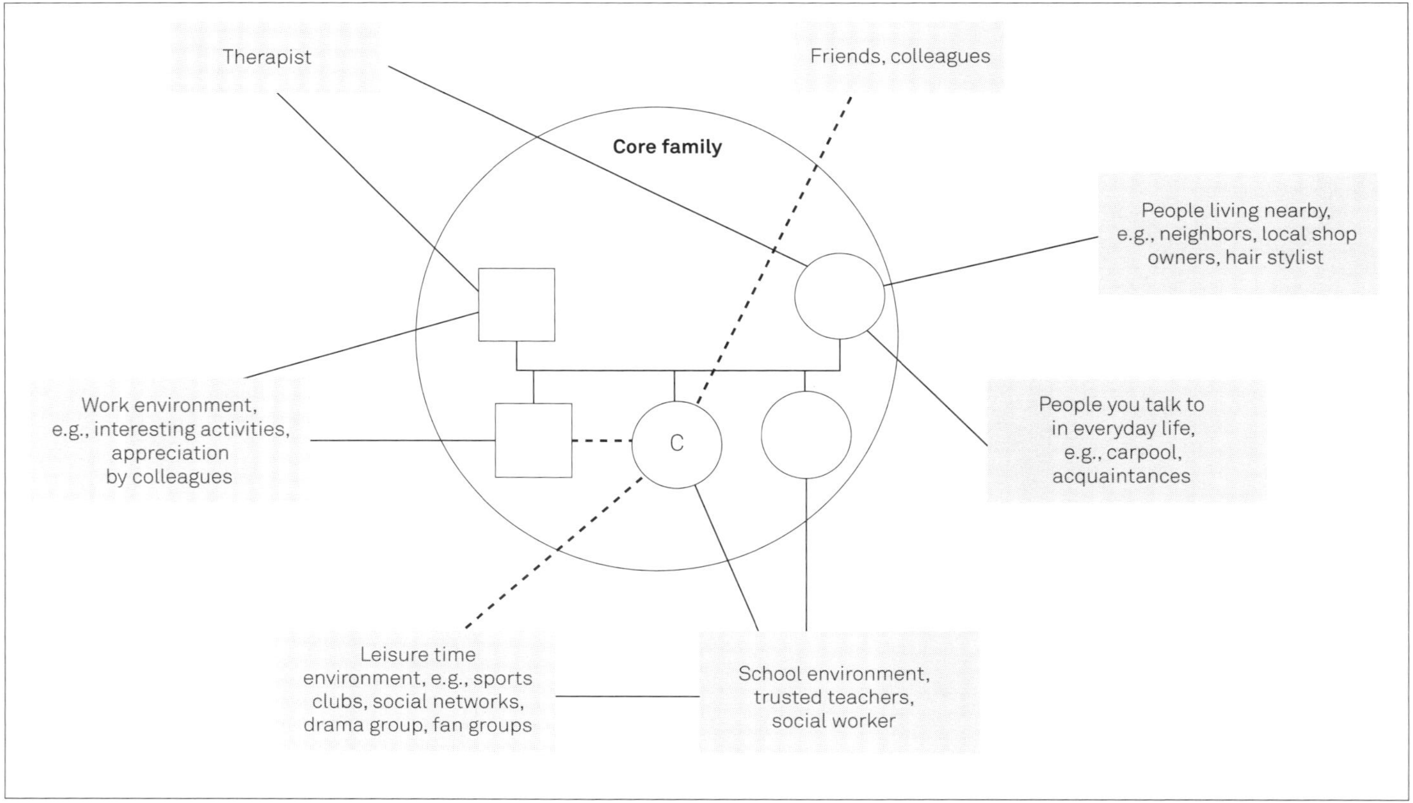

Figure 8. Social network from a resource perspective, with the current core family (oval in the middle) and the extended social context. C = client. Dotted lines denote social links perceived as resources by the client, solid lines denote additional social links.

Enhancing Social Imagery

People seeking support in therapy rarely suffer from having too many resources, skills, abilities, and joy in life, but typically due to unresolved life problems, precarious life situations, or other adverse circumstances. Therefore, it is not surprising that the resources of clients quickly disappear from the focus of psychotherapeutic interventions simply due to empathetic resonance. It is all the more important that therapists actively incorporate resources into the therapeutic process on their own. All the methods in this book are dedicated to this goal. Humans are "social animals" (Baumeister, 2005): They can only experience most of what they want to do in social spaces, networks, or relationships. They are thus socially embedded. Or, in extreme cases, would hardly be able to survive without any human social experience. In family and couples therapy, but also individual therapy, social resources are utilized in a variety of ways, be it through the direct involvement of significant others or by using therapy as a social space. For example, couples can support each other more intensively (Falconier et al., 2015). Social resources are the key resources in successful change or therapy processes. The support received in counseling or therapy can become part of the experience of social resources in the life space of the person seeking advice. Another central (interpersonal) ability of humans is their ability to learn and adapt. Learning and adaptability are fundamental achievements that have developed over the course of evolution and are directly linked to language acquisition and spatial-temporal imagination. Compared to their animal counterparts, humans are relatively inept at flying, climbing, swimming, running, or biting; the only evolutionary advantage they offer is their exceptional learning ability, which preferably occurs in social contexts – for instance, thinking in a specific socially learned language. It is worthwhile to sufficiently focus on the activation of social networks in counseling and therapy. The representation of social systems tends to become complex. Genograms and ecograms offer good opportunities to develop an overview of the social system. The activation of social networks as resources can be further deepened. Central here, is the notion that social resources do not merely wither as purely verbalized information units but are activated as comprehensive cognitive-motivational-emotional imagery in the sense of mental simulation (Bagheri et al, 2024).

Imagery has the following characteristics:

- Mental simulation of concrete situations.
- Focus on emotional experience.
- Inclusion of visual representations.
- Elaboration of individual meanings.

- Condensation of statements or experiences.
- Inclusion of autobiographical learning history.

Resources in the sense of mental imagery enable resource transfer. They are emotionally perceivable, can be initiated with key stimuli, and thus are available in situations where they are needed as coping resources. For exploring or deepening social resources, the following questions might be helpful:
- In which relationships do you experience resources? In which social situations can this be experienced?
- What physical sensations are associated with it?
- Are there important shared experiences?
- What feelings and sensations are associated with the perception of the social resource?
- Can the perceived resource be connected to a bodily feeling, an action, or an exemplary image?
- Is it possible/sensible to make this resource more accessible in everyday life?
- Is a change in the current experience noticeable with the perception of the social resource?
- With whom can you talk about certain resources?
- With whom do you discuss your personal experiences that make you happy, give you confidence, make you proud, or provide life meaning? – What impact will the resources have on your own life in the near future?

Further Reading

Baumeister, R. F. (2005). *The cultural animal: Human nature, meaning, and social life*. Oxford University Press. https://doi.org/10.1093/acprof:oso/9780195167030.001.0001

Systematizing Change

One of the most remarkable findings in psychotherapy research is that 60–80% of depressed outpatients experience a rapid and stable improvement in symptoms within the first five sessions (Shalom & Aderka, 2020). These improvements can be systematically addressed and utilized for therapy. Often, therapists briefly address these improvements at the beginning of therapy. However, the improvements are often explored in a superficial and unsystematized way and not sufficiently utilized for further therapy. Dedicate an intensive 10 to 15 minutes at the beginning of a session to explore changes/improvements – it will be worthwhile for the session's progression.

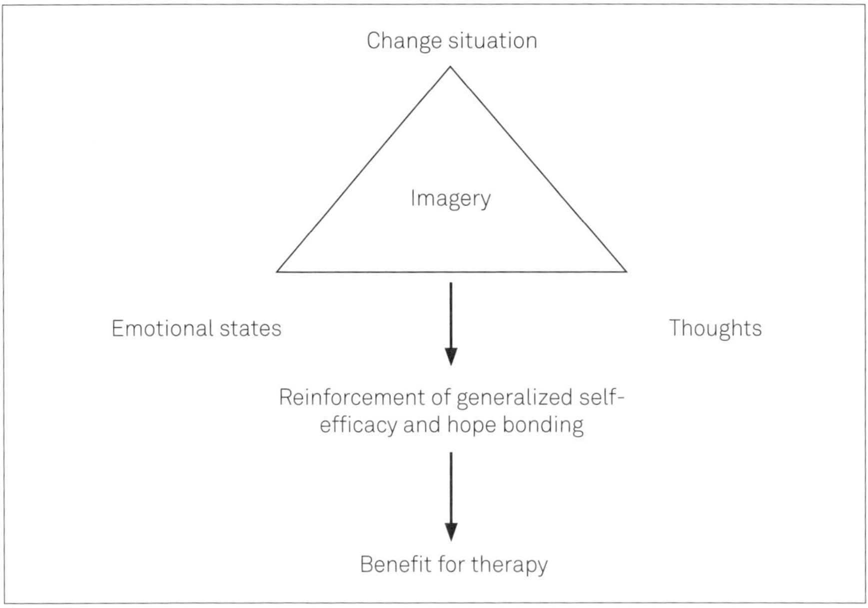

Figure 9. Exploration of a change situation for about 10–15 minutes during a session.

Figure 9 provides an overview of a complete exploration cycle (also available as Handout 4 in the Appendix) and the six different elements of a cycle are discussed in more detail in the following.

Exploration of a detailed picture of how change occurred in a particular situation: Explore until you can vividly imagine the change situation. Possible exploratory questions:

- What exactly has changed? What is the timeline?
- How did you first notice the changes? How was the first change recognized? Identify the initial trigger of the change.
- What were your own (action) contributions? Did you have to do something for the change, or was it more a shift in the focus of attention?

Exploration of emotions and feelings: Address the feelings that arose during the change situation. Start with an open question:

Has your emotional experience altered as a result of your change?

- Recognize and possibly differentiate positive feelings (such as joy, pride, relief, calmness, courage). Mentioning positive feelings is often associated with shame. By addressing what makes us proud, we also make ourselves vulnerable.

- Exploration of possible painful feelings, like sadness/frustration, that the situation did not change for so long.

Exploration of helpful thoughts: Facing a difficult situation is often associated with positive thoughts and helpful self-verbalizations. Develop a detailed picture of how the patient communicated with themselves during the change situation.
- Identify automatic positive thoughts like "See, it works," "You can do it," "I'll show them," "Just wait."
- Develop relevant self-verbalizations that enabled mastering the situation, like "Come what may, just get up," "I know what to do."
- Identify helpful thoughts that checkmated fears, like "I might feel afraid and notice that it automatically fades without needing to fight it," "Dear fears, it's okay that you're here with me, but you can take a break for a few minutes as I need to focus on the action now."

Positive imagery: Situational action, emotional experience, and exemplary thoughts are directly interconnected and usually occur simultaneously. For further therapy progression, it may be helpful to give the improvement or exception a clear name or a metaphor, making it easily retrievable at a later point in time.

Reinforcement of generalized self-efficacy and hope bonding: Improvements have immediate significance for future work in therapy:
- Assure that things are changeable.
- Reinforce the patient's self-efficacy expectations by developing positive therapy-related thoughts like "You can give yourself chances," "Small steps lead to change," "Practice makes perfect."
- Address any external attributions and identify the patient's contributions.
- In the change situation, gather possible earlier obstacles and killer arguments. Assure that these automatic negative fears retrospectively appear smaller.
- Address any improvement/change pressure. Illustrate that not everything has to change at once ("Everything has its time"). Point out that the pace of the change process is adjustable.

Benefit for therapy: Initial changes can now be associated with the still-existing problematic aspects. Can individual elements (such as positive self-verbalizations) also be applied to other problematic areas? Furthermore, addressing possible setbacks is essentially a sign of a usual learning curve! Possible difficulties identifying initial changes is generally a joyful and optimistic task. Try to appreciate and non-verbally support the patient's (often silent) joy with detailed inquiries. The goal is not to exuberantly push small changes onto the patient. Your positive mood should not be reinforced, but rather the patient's. Therefore, try to explore very precisely to understand the changes as closely to behavior as possible. Ensure that initial changes can accompany negative feelings such as stress, sadness, or anger. Do not leave the patient alone in these aspects. Avoid the meta-message that only a patient who makes quick changes and euphorically reports them is a "good" patient. The aim is not to socialize patients into becoming "performers" for therapy.

Further Reading

Flückiger, C., Holtforth, M. G., Del Re, A. C., & Lutz, W. (2013). Working along sudden gains: Responsiveness on small and subtle early changes and exceptions. *Psychotherapy, 50*(3), 292–297. https://doi.org/10.1037/a0031940

Elaborated Goal-Orientation Using the Example of Miracle Questions

Resource-activating interventions expand the scope of action that patients can create; it is therefore a form of goal-oriented psychotherapy. This sets in place a process of change that begins with a goal. The basic idea is that, in addition to understanding problematic aspects, it is particularly relevant how target states can be desired, dreamed of and longed for. Understanding and exploring the target states will help to take the first steps in the desired direction and shift the focus of attention away from preventing negative states (De Shazer, 1988).

Procedure

Before asking the miracle questions, the therapist or counselor should prepare the patient for it, e.g., "I'd like to ask you a slightly unusual question ... if that's OK with you. (...) I'd like to ask you – before I move on to the question – even if this question may seem a bit bizarre – to answer it as precisely as you can. You might feel as if you can't answer it at all. But I'd like you to give it a try anyway. Are you OK with that?" Asking the patient for permission prepares them for an intervention. The patient is given the opportunity to influence the course of the conversation, making counseling or therapy a mutual process. Miracle questions can be asked in different ways, but they should always relate to the patients' experience. A few examples:

- "Let's assume that tonight, while you're asleep, a miracle happens, and the problems you're discussing here are all solved. But because you're asleep you don't know that a miracle has occurred. Tomorrow morning, however, after getting up, you realize something's changed. What could that be? What would you notice? When would you realize that the miracle has happened? What would you do? What would indicate to other people that something has changed?"
- "You go on a trip round the world. During the journey, which takes you to all corners of the world, to your surprise three events you've been wishing for a long time occur. How would you feel after the events? What happened? What is different afterwards? What is missing while the events are going on? What is the impact of the events on your problems?"
- "Imagine you meet a fairy godmother. She offers you the opportunity to strip away three of your current problems. When you wake the next morning, the problems are gone. What would change? Who would first notice it? How would others react to the change? What would you do, and what would be different now?"
- "Most people wish for specific things: 'If I could, only once, get what I want, I'd . . .' What would you do if only once you could get what you wanted? Feel free to be unrealistic. What are your wishes, what images or events do you picture in your mind's eye when you imagine a moment of unadulterated joy? What would be happening? Are other people there? What is your reaction? What is their reaction? How did the whole thing start – before the event occurred? Think of it: Every journey starts with the first step outside your own door. What would your first step look like?"
- "On TV, they are planning a piece about you. It will introduce you to a broader audience. What would it say about you? What would other people think of said piece? What would viewers think of your life (exciting, quiet, dramatic)? What would other people say about your life, and how would you feel about that?"
- "Imagine we meet again in 5 years' time. Your life has gone exactly the way you were hoping it would. You've solved the problems you're here for today to your complete satisfaction. You could say you're in a situation where you feel completely at ease. What would you appear like to me? How would your life have changed in the meantime? How did the change occur? What would such a situation look like?"

Miracle questions can be adapted to suit the patient's individual preferences. Depending on what basic needs are relevant to them at that point in time, the miracle question can be asked in connection with a specific need.

With the help of miracle questions, the patient can work out a global target vision. In the subsequent processing phase, it is important to delineate the vision more clearly. The patient should draw up a plan on how to approximate the target vision: The vision serves as a signpost, and the plan supports the material implementation of the goals aimed for. Placing visions in a hierarchy of goals, partial goals, and micro-goals can prove useful. Micro-goals are goals the person can immediately start implementing in daily life without building new behavioral patterns: They take, as it were, micro-steps in the right direction.

Possible questions for delineating the target visions:

- What would it be like if the problem didn't exist anymore?
- What would you notice first?
- Who besides yourself would first notice that the problem is gone – and how would they notice?

Fulfilling these goals should be possible over the course of therapy. As a rule, one should think in terms of micro-steps. The therapist should always discuss together with the patient whether the goals are realistic. Eventually the patient should receive instructions that are as precise as possible as to how to go about achieving those goals.

Potential Difficulties

Big and important-sounding words such as visions, miracles, or life goals may be perceived as hyperbolic. As mentioned above, the introduction should suit the person's life situation. It is helpful and beneficial if the therapist adopts the patient's language and includes individual images, words, or expressions in the miracle questions. A business manager has a "clear" idea, develops the "perfect project" in a "think tank." "Fairies" and "magicians" are clearly allowed only when they are part of the person's life situation.

Further Reading

Willutzki, U., & Koban, C. (2004). Enhancing motivation for psychotherapy: The elaboration of eositive eerspectives (EPOS) to develop clients' goal structure. In W. M. Cox & E. Klinger (Eds.), *Handbook of motivational counseling: Concepts, approaches, and assessment* (pp. 337–356). John Wiley & Sons Ltd.

Vermeulen-Oskam, E., Franklin, C., Hof, L. P. M. V., Stams, G. J. J. M., Van Vugt, E. S., Assink, M., Veltman, E. J., Froerer, A. S., Staaks, J. P. C., & Zhang, A. (2024). The current evidence of solution-focused brief therapy: A meta-analysis of psychosocial outcomes and moderating factors. *Clinical Psychology Review, 114*, Article 102512. https://doi.org/10.1016/j.cpr.2024.102512

Other People as Resource Models

Other people are useful as examples when they are accepted as role models, and when they possess skills that are useful to the patient. At the same time, the model behavior derived from the role model should not be too far removed, to avoid the patient perceiving it as unattainable (Bandura, 1986).

Procedure

This kind of intervention starts with the following central questions:
- Do you know someone who possesses exactly those resources that would be necessary to you in a specific context?
- How does that person behave in similar situations?
- What do they do differently?
- Have you ever behaved similarly to your role model?
- What would others in your life, such as your partner, say?
- When did you ever behave in a similar way to your role model?

The patient should experience their resources in an unmediated way: They should not talk about skills and talent without activating them in their natural context. It is therefore necessary for the patient to get a clear idea of the role model's resources. The following interventions can contribute to delineating the resource activation:
- Imagine the situation. Take on your model's role. What would be your thoughts? What feelings would arise in you?
- What do you expect would happen?
- What feelings is this expectation tied to?
- What can you see?
- What are you focusing your attention on?
- What words and sentences would you utter now?
- What would you do now?

Doing "homework" is also useful to experiment and practice the behavior. The patient should try to behave similarly to their role model. When assessing the homework the therapist can ask the following questions:
- What did you do in that situation?
- What was going through your head as you were behaving like that?
- How did you feel in that situation?
- What affected you afterwards?
- What were the consequences of your behavior?
- Did something about your attitude change?

Potential Difficulties

One of the main difficulties is that patients make demands on themselves they cannot live up to. Thus, when deciding on the homework, the therapist has to make sure that the patients do not set unrealistic tasks for themselves. The behavioral goal should be achievable. Micro-steps are again the key. It is better to take a micro-step than not to take a giant one.

Further Reading

Cottle, J., Drozdik, A. L., & Rimes, K. A. (2024). The impact of role models and mentors on the mental and physical wellbeing of sexual and gender minorities. *Behavioral Sciences, 14*(5), Article 417. https://doi.org/10.3390/bs14050417

Scott, W. D., Cervone, D., & Ebiringah, O. U. (2024). The social-cognitive clinician: On the implications of social cognitive theory for psychotherapy and assessment. *International Journal of Psychology, 59*(5), 616–623. https://doi.org/10.1002/ijop.13125

Activating Coping Resources Through Role Reversal

The following intervention works well when the patient is ready to face the problem or when the problem seems to have reached a dead end: The patient and therapist swap roles, turning the patient into his or her own therapist. The role reversal allows patients to distance themselves from their own situation, which makes them activate their own solution competencies.

Procedure

Role reversal can be developed out of the therapeutic process without having to invest too much effort. For instance, "I am under the impression that the situation has become stagnant. I'd like to understand that more clearly. Would you care to describe the problem more clearly?" The therapist works out the patient's central thoughts, emotions, and behaviors in the problem situation until they feel they can describe those behaviors, thoughts, and emotions in detail. The therapist now repeats the central thoughts and emotions and describes the behaviors that are part of the problem situation. Subsequently, the therapist asks the patient if it is OK to deal with this situation in more detail: "Are you OK with our dealing with this in more detail?" If the patient does agree, the therapist can continue the intervention as described below. One advantage of the exercise is how simple it is to integrate it into the process. Role play enables a high degree of emotional activation, and at the same time, the patient's solution and coping competencies are also activated. The patient is freed from their role as the bearer of the problem. In addition, the intervention serves as an ideal link between coping with the problem and activating resources – and it is a good example of how those two components can be interwoven in the clinical process to achieve the desired effect. The process is described in its entirety below.

1. *Exploring the problem situation:* moving from the situation to the emotion and cognition;
2. *Summarizing and working out:* the nagging thought as the central element and possibly an indication as to how convinced the patient is there of;
3. *Asking permission* to deal with the problem in more detail;
4. *Role reversal:* For role reversal it can be useful for the therapist and patient to physically swap seats, which makes taking over the new role easier. "Imagine a friend relates the following problem . . ." The therapist takes on the patient's role and describes the difficulties and problems the patient has been talking about. While doing so, the therapist tries to communicate the central cognitions and emotions connected with the experience of the problem situation, which potentially can be condensed into a central statement. As far as possible the therapist should use the patient's own language. After the therapist's describing the problem in the role of the patient, the patient asks him or her questions in the role of the therapist: "How would you respond to that?" Instead of a partner, other confidants can be introduced – a brother, a sister, or a work colleague. Who is chosen depends on the individual case. Merely picturing that other person having a similar problem can sometimes be a relief in itself.
5. *Checking the viability:* test the viability of the suggestions through careful objection, not necessarily by immediately accepting the first suggestion, but by allowing for ambivalence, exposing target conflicts, not disrupting the solution. Tread carefully and "immunize" through a careful "yes-but" game.
6. *Returning to the old roles:* The seats are swapped back, and both persons return to their original roles. The therapist can now query about the role reversal: "As therapist you just suggested a few strong potential solutions. Do some of the suggestions you made apply to you as well?" The therapist can now work things out by pointing to changes emerging from the role reversal. Attitudes may have changed, convictions questioned, alternative behaviors suggested; or they could be complementary thoughts and newly perceived emotions.
7. *Evaluation:* Finally, the therapist can ask: "How sure are you at the moment of the original central sentence?"

Potential Difficulties

While clinical practice shows that this exercise can activate numerous fears in the therapist, it can still usually be carried out very well. One difficulty may be that the patient categorically refuses the role reversal. A resource-oriented response to this behavior could be: "You can always say what you want to do and what you don't want to do, this is a vital skill. We can deal with the problem in another way."

A second difficulty may arise over time if the patient cannot think of any alternative ideas while in the role of the therapist. Patients might fail to find solutions as long as they consider themselves uniquely abnormal. In that case, the therapist can try to amplify the appeal for help in the role of the patient, which then often activates ideas for solutions.

Clinical experience shows that patients who embrace the intervention also develop helpful ideas for solutions in the role of the therapist.

Further Reading

Pugh, M. (2019). *Cognitive behavioural chairwork: Distinctive features*. Routledge. https://doi.org/10.4324/9780429023927

Pascual-Leone, A., & Baher, T. (2023). Chairwork in individual psychotherapy: Meta-analyses of intervention effects. *Psychotherapy, 60*(3), 370–382. https://doi.org/10.1037/pst0000490

Bell, T., Dixon, A., & Kolts, R. (2016). Developing a compassionate internal supervisor: Compassion-focused therapy for trainee therapists. *Clinical Psychology & Psychotherapy, 24*(3), 632–648. https://doi.org/10.1002/cpp.2031

Planning Pleasure

The interventions discussed in this chapter aim to boost pleasant sensations and activate them as perception. The question is whether pleasure can in fact be learned or trained at all. Pleasure "training" implies not only the pleasure itself, but also some amount of effort, which would seem to be the opposite of something enjoyable. Below we do not deal with how to heighten the ability to feel pleasure; rather we invite you to follow the individual tracks that lead to the experience of pleasant sensations. Sensitizing the patient's senses seeks to create positive experiences that run counter to those they experience at the beginning of the therapy.

Procedure

1. *Planning pleasure:* Consciousness is a precondition to learning how to feel pleasure again – in other words, conscious pleasure. The patient/client should have the time and opportunity to direct their attention to feeling pleasure. In order to create the proper spatial and situational conditions necessary for pleasure, one must have a plan: The time and the situation must be created. What can be enjoyed and how it is enjoyed depends more on the patient's experiential background. Normally, it can be assumed that people are able to reflect back on enjoyable experiences they had during their lifetime. It is useful to refer to these. The first step for the patient is to learn that pleasure is preceded by a phase in which pleasure is set up, by actively creating the conditions that are relevant to an enjoyable experience. This preparation phase is not only a necessary precondition, but it can also become enjoyable in and of itself. The boundary between the preparation and the start of the actual pleasure is at best blurred.
2. *Time and duration:* The time for experiencing the enjoyable action and how long it ought to last, should be planned. Often people say that they do not have the time to enjoy themselves. This is the crux of the matter: They hinder themselves in doing so. This is not an argument against pleasure as such, but rather underlines the importance of effectively planning pleasure. Not only when patients are to enjoy themselves, should this be considered, but also how long, i.e., that there is also an end to said enjoyable event.

Potential Difficulties

What is pleasant? What does a person perceive as pleasurable? Many actions may be deemed pleasurable because they are accompanied by pleasant thoughts or feelings. With clinically depressed patients, this point is inextricably tied to the vicious circle of depression. Events or changes perceived by the patient in the past as pleasant can offer a clue to enjoyable actions.

If the patient primarily mentions passive behavior when asked about pleasant actions, e.g., watching TV, it is vital to determine the attending thoughts and feelings. Of course, watching TV is a perfectly enjoyable activity; however, if a depressed patient watches TV with the thought: "Here I am again in front of the TV, that's boring. All I do is slouch around . . .," then that is certainly not pleasurable. Whether something is enjoyable or not can be checked against the thoughts and sensations of the person during the action. This check is important if the preparation of the enjoyable action is to lead to something that is in fact enjoyable.

The therapist should try to find out together with the patient what is pleasurable. Possible questions are:

- What kind of pleasure is allowed and what kind isn't allowed?
- What do you like right now?
- What can you imagine achieving?
- Are there areas that you picture as being pleasant, but haven't delved into yet?

What is good and what is not good comes down to the patient. In that sense, it is important to know what is pleasant, but it is equally important to know what is unpleasant and what the person does not want.

What Does it Mean to "Really Enjoy" Something?

It is important to communicate to the patient that there is no right or wrong about pleasure. Pleasure exercises can lead to experiences that are more or less pleasant. Learning to feel pleasure means practicing to feel pleasure. One cannot *not* feel pleasure. All people can differentiate between pleasant and unpleasant sensations. When feeling pleasure, it is important to locate those sensations that are pleasant and thus steer toward having more pleasant than unpleasant experiences.

If pleasure becomes a taboo, experiencing pleasure can become very difficult. Sexuality, for instance, is a taboo area for many people. The extent to which pleasure is accepted or forbidden is highly dependent on one's family history. Family upbringing is the first normative authority that imparts how and where something can be perceived as pleasurable – or not. Rigid family rules can inhibit the perception of pleasurable sensations.

Further Reading

Abel, D. B., Rand, K. L., Salyers, M. P., Myers, E. J., Mickens, J. L., & Minor, K. S. (2023). Do people with schizophrenia enjoy social activities as much as everyone else? A meta-analysis of consummatory social pleasure. *Schizophrenia Bulletin, 49*(3), 809–822. https://doi.org/10.1093/schbul/sbac199

Zaneva, M., Philpott, A., Singh, A., Larsson, G., & Gonsalves, L. (2022). What is the added value of incorporating pleasure in sexual health interventions? A systematic review and meta-analysis. *PLoS ONE, 17*(2), Article e0261034. https://doi.org/10.1371/journal.pone.0261034

Resource Activation Through Imaginative Procedures

In order to improve the patient's well-being, relaxation techniques can be helpful. In many cases, a change in the patient's level of tension and an increase in their well-being can be achieved in a short time. Choose a method that suits the patient's individual preconditions, for example, relaxation exercises from the progressive muscle relaxation technique, hypnotherapy, or imaginative procedures. The procedure we investigate in more detail below is based on the imagination method.

Imaginative procedures allow the therapist to use images during relaxation in order to enhance the patient's mood and to directly activate their positive emotions.

Procedure

Introducing a patient to an imagination exercise might look something like this:

> I'd now like to try out a little exercise with you. It's a relaxation exercise. Some of this may feel unfamiliar, but remember it is just an offer: You can't do anything right or wrong. If you feel like it, you can choose to stop the exercise at any moment. However, it's possible that some of the instructions might in fact work for you, and you'll want to follow them. You might notice that certain objects or certain images help you relax, whereas others may not. Just follow those aspects of the exercise that help you relax. Perhaps you don't feel any noticeable relaxation, in which case just be open to what is happening. That doesn't mean that you've done something wrong. Our experiences with relaxation exercises show that everyone has an individual reaction to them. Are you ready to begin? Do you have any questions? OK, well, let's start, then.

The exercise should not be too long; for some patients this kind of exercise is completely new, and they might feel insecure about it. The first attempt at imagination or relaxation exercises should last no longer than 15 minutes. If the patient experiences the exercise as positive, a longer imagination exercise may be carried out in a follow-up session. Once the patient is receptive, the therapist can start the imagination exercise (see Box 1). Talk slowly and make sure there are enough pauses.

Box 1. A Place of Quietude and Strength

Find a comfortable position and try to relax as best you can. Find a position and a spot in this room that will allow you to really relax. You might want to change the position of the chair, you might want to sit or lie down. Your gaze can be directed in the room or out the window. Try out what the most comfortable position is for you. Take your time. Sometimes you think you've found the right position, but suddenly you feel the impulse to change your position again. Give yourself permission to do so. The change may be big or small, maybe only the position of your feet or hands, head or neck. Sometimes a small movement can in fact help the body relax further. Allow your body to find the position where it can continue to relax further and further. Even after a while you may realize that a certain posture or position isn't as comfortable as you initially thought. Feel free to change it again. Your body will find a position in which it feels entirely comfortable. Try and make everything around you unimportant. Dismiss for a short while, all objects, words, events that previously seemed so very important so that you can get in touch with yourself. Notice how the air flows into your body and back out, how your breath carries you. Notice it but without changing anything, how your body takes care of you, breath after breath. If you want to, close your eyes and focus on yourself, on your own breathing. The air flows in and out, just like that, by itself. Maybe there's a short pause after each breath – allow it: It is your body recovering. And while you're lying or sitting there and relaxing further and further, pictures may begin to appear before your mind's eye. At first maybe it's just dots, patterns, or color images. The images might stay a while or go away again. They might be sharp or blurred. Maybe they change or morph. Just allow what is happening in your mind's eye to happen. You may be surprised at all the things you can see with your eyes closed. Maybe one of the images is particularly pleasurable. Try and stay with it, look at it. Notice where you are. Who else is there? Is there a specific smell? Or taste? An event or situation, maybe it's inside or outside? Is it warm or cold? Maybe you can feel the temperature on your skin. Look around you and absorb the image. Seeing, smelling, tasting, hearing, feeling. Taking it all in with all your senses, notice it and savor it.

Enjoy the pleasurable and agreeable feeling of energy and relaxation. Of just being here and taking in this place of quietude, strength, and relaxation. Feel it and allow it to affect you. Enjoy it and absorb it, the energy and strength. Take something with you from this place, like a souvenir from a trip. Then you can go back anytime you want. And now slowly say good-bye to this place, notice how the air is still flowing into your body and back out, just like that. Take all the time you need to come back, to this room. Allow your body to take what it needs, maybe you want to stretch, run your hands across your face. To be here again in this room, and open your eyes.

Potential Difficulties

When assessing the exercise afterward, it is important to process what the patient experienced during the process. The therapist should remain open to the patient's experiences. With a patient who says that they couldn't really get into the exercise, it is important that the therapist emphasize the patient's active contributions, for instance, that they didn't resist it, or that they tried to actively do the exercise. It is important to evaluate even this experience in depth. The therapist may want to point out the subjectivity of the experience. If patients denigrate themselves, thinking "I can't do this," the following explanation may prove helpful: "I think you actively embraced this new exercise. If you feel now that you can't do this, this might just have to do with the fact that it is something new and is unfamiliar to you. And it's perfectly normal not to know how to do unfamiliar things. It's like sports: Remember what it was like when you first stood on skis. You probably were a bit un- steady on your feet. Relaxation is very similar. But if you're interested in it and you try and relax regularly, you will notice over time that you can experience new and different things."

With this exercise, as with all other interventions described in this book, it is important that the therapist emphasize the patient's active contributions, in order to give them a sense of their own activity. The therapist should, whenever possible, enable the client to become more aware of their own "actions." Whenever the client gains a better sense of their own activity, they also become more aware of their own resources.

Practice makes perfect, as the old saying goes. The therapist should encourage the patient to do the relaxation exercise on their own before the next session. You may want to give the patient a taped recording of it.

Further Reading

Schürmann-Vengels, J., Victor, P. P., Odyniec, P., Flückiger, C., Teismann, T., & Willutzki, U. (2022). A mental imagery micro-intervention to increase positive affect in outpatient CBT sessions (PACIfIC): Study protocol of a randomized controlled implementation trial. *Clinical Psychology in Europe, 4*(2), Article e7043. https://doi.org/10.32872/cpe.7043

Resource Diary

The function of diaries, among other things, is to identify relationships the person may only vaguely be aware of and whose signposts are not clearly recognizable. In the treatment of depression, for instance, a diary may demonstrate the relationship between positive events and positive moods. Structured resource diaries can refer to broader areas, including social support, individual skills and talents, i.e., all areas with potential resource hotspots (Chapter 1) and resource perspectives (Chapter 2). These could be specific thematic areas that are dealt with in more depth during therapy or in a broader focus, to highlight events that would normally be deemed unimportant or negligible.

Procedure

The choice of resource areas has to be made, so as to monitor everyday events:
1) Define the resource areas to be documented in the following week.
2) Define a response format (e.g., situation, event, mood, personal resource).

Potential Difficulties

The areas monitored have to be specific enough to be useful within the individual case formulation. The focus should hence not be placed on what the individual is already aware of, but rather on what is located in the gray area of the semiconsciousness. Criticism along the lines of "Oh, I understand all that" can be countered by pointing out that a full understanding of unproblematic areas can be helpful in understanding problematic aspects.

Further Reading

Reiter, C., & Wilz, G. (2015). Resource diary: A positive writing intervention for promoting well-being and preventing depression in adolescence. *The Journal of Positive Psychology, 11*(1), 99–108. https://doi.org/10.1080/17439760.2015.1025423

Differentiating Between Positive Feelings and Moods

At a high level of abstraction, affective experience can be placed in one of two categories – positive or negative affect. Patients often generalize their emotional state in strongly abstract terms and even upon repeated questioning hardly ever differentiate ("Today I'm just great!" or "Last week I felt like crap!"). Traditionally, psychotherapy and counseling have been geared to understanding the generation of negative affect (e.g., by means of situational analysis, an in-depth review, or the discovery of automatic negative thoughts). But these methods can also be applied with a view toward discovering positive experiences, with the goal being of becoming more aware of positive affective experience.

Procedure

Handout 3 (see Appendix) allows one to become aware of and gain an overview of the spectrum of positive affect. Collating different situations from the recent and distant past connected to a specific positive mood serves to emphasize the quality and strength of positive experience. Not only highly intense "one-off" events are of significance; everyday events must be considered as well. Using mood questionnaires can sharpen a patient's awareness of their current mood.

Potential Difficulties

The person may only remember situations from the distant past and regret not experiencing such things anymore. If this is the case, it is vital to look for situations that enable the person to experience positive affects in their everyday life – even if only to a small degree.

Further Reading

Craske, M. G., Meuret, A. E., Echiverri-Cohen, A., Rosenfield, D., & Ritz, T. (2023). Positive affect treatment targets reward sensitivity: A randomized controlled trial. *Journal of Consulting and Clinical Psychology, 91*(6), 350–366. https://doi.org/10.1037/ccp0000805

Stalikas, A., & Fitzpatrick, M. R. (2008). Positive emotions in psychotherapy theory, research, and practice: New kid on the block? *Journal of Psychotherapy Integration, 18*(2), 155–166. https://doi.org/10.1037/1053-0479.18.2.155

Reframing and Normalization

The effect of positive reassessment (reframing) and normalization on a specific person or target group is as specific and cultural as a good joke. The aim of reframing is to make problems more manageable – to qualify and to contain them. Reframing can come in the shape of metaphors, stories, and allegories. The insurmountable problems the patient faces can thereby lose some of their menace and complexity. Usually, situations may be found in a person's biography in which the problem behavior they have acquired was useful or even crucial to their survival. Problem behavior is hence not inherently problematic but merely applied at the wrong time. The way events are perceived as well as their attendant attitudes and value systems make up the individual way of absorbing and processing information. Nearly every problem has positive sides. The aim of reframing is for the patient to re-evaluate things: to allow for the problem to be accessed from its positive angle. A patient seeing previous behavior as exclusively problematic can now detect a new meaning to the behavior with the help of such reassessments. It is purely irrational, as the patient used to think, but it can now be read within a specific situational context that has certain effects – and mostly positive ones at that. The patient is often amazed at such reassessments. Reframing is a question of the specific therapy situation, particularly the therapy style. It cannot be divorced from clear therapeutic convictions and is an intention on the part of the therapist to see the patient from his or her most positive side.

Procedure

It can be helpful to set up a card index of possible reframing tailored to the target group. Table 3 gives a few examples of common reframing and normalizations.

Table 3. Possible reframing and normalizations

Problem aspect	Reframe into	Positive behavior
Sensitive	→	Alert, attentive
Fearful	→	Being concerned about yourself, only those who are afraid need a lot of courage
Withdrawn	→	Considerate, discreet
Envious	→	Knowing what you want
Jealous	→	Protecting the source of one's own relationship needs
Arrogant	→	Knowing how to maintain distance
Confused	→	Realizing that there are many possibilities out there
Aggressive	→	Fighting for your own goals
Pigheaded	→	Self-assertive and self-confident
Worthless	→	Nothing is without value
Depressed	→	Melancholy can suggest deep understanding
Mistrustful	→	Careful
Tense	→	Full of energy
Docile	→	Being open to compromise
Hurt	→	Time for healing
Vulnerable	→	We're all vulnerable
Sensitive	→	Being able to empathize

Try and add positive synonyms to negative attributes with the help of the word thesaurus when you're working on the concept for a case or a case report – and then reread your report!

Of course, some events can't be reframed in a few words, but need the help of metaphors:

- Therapy can sometimes be like a mountain hike: We travel together, but you must walk on your own.
- School, training, or studies are like a marathon: Being head of the class in year 1 is not enough; you need to have the stamina to stick it out until the end.
- If you roll a 1 three times in a row, it is (mathematically) unfair, of course, but in the end, it might turn out to be a blessing ...
- You don't want to change depending on the game. OK, just try it.

Potential Difficulties

Reframing can tell you what the therapist is thinking and how far the clients are willing to go down the road toward reassessment. Reframing is thus also always shaped by one's perception and the therapist's own background. Nevertheless, the aim of reframing is to obtain a better, more complete patient's understanding of oneself. It can be helpful if the therapist adopts some of the patient's images, words, and metaphors.

Further Reading

Murphy, J. J. (2023). *Solution-focused therapy*. American Psychological Association. https://doi.org/10.1037/0000370-000

Character Strengths

Psychotherapy patients are often very successful in focusing on the things they want to avoid (e.g., preventing their son from leaving the house without brushing their teeth, preventing them from dying in fear of death, preventing arguments). The perfidious thing about this avoidance mode is that attention is focused on the very thing that you actually want to prevent. As a metaphorical example, you may be familiar with the unpleasant feeling of driving over a narrow bridge. If you move your head back and forth between the two crash barriers to make sure you don't crash directly into them, you may lose your orientation and stop. If you fixate on the end point, you will probably find the middle between the two crash barriers better and drive off gently. Practically all schools of psychotherapy do not only ask themselves what psychotherapy wants to prevent (e.g., fewer symptoms, less sadness, less fatigue, less anxiety), but also the question of human goals. Questions about one's own life goals and wishes are often asked by patients in the second half of therapy, and an initial reduction in stress factors offers a little more freedom again. Lists of values, needs or character offer a possibility to deal with one's own long-term human goals.

Procedure

The list of character strengths in Box 2 (Niemiec, 2018), which was developed within the framework of positive psychology (Peterson & Seligman, 2004), shows various human traits (also available as Handout 5 in the Appendix). If there is an explicit therapy assignment, this list can be used to reflect on further (life) goals in therapy and to consider a longer-term perspective that goes beyond the actual phase of therapy and poses the question of meaning in one's own life. After a brief introduction, ask an open question. For example: Which point particularly appeals to you? Which point amazes you? Is there a point that you find particularly easy? Is a point missing? Is a point annoying? Try to steer the conversation with the patient towards in-depth (self-) reflection. Try to concretize, comprehend, and understand the meaning of situations (e.g., Where exactly do you find the point in question? Where not?). Try to make the conversation more protracted, and make the emotional and motivational meaning directly perceptible and tangible for the patient.

Possible Difficulties

Avoid leading questions. At best, offer two or three alternatives. The individual character strengths are relatively abstractly formulated. Try to break through the surface of the conversation by reflecting on the individual meanings in the patient's experience and behavior. What is relevant is not the amount of character strengths, but their emotional-motivational significance for the patient. Try to explore them as behaviorally as possible by discussing concrete examples. Try to set a concrete goal for the near future. This can be in the form of a homework assignment and can include both an observation task and smaller behavioral experiments.

Further Reading

Niemiec, R. M. (2018). *Character strengths interventions.* Hogrefe.

Box 2. List of 24 Character Strengths

Wisdom

Wisdom goes beyond lexical knowledge and relates to a person's entire life experience.

1. Creativity – finding new solutions
2. Curiosity – being interested
3. Judgment – weighing things up carefully; being open-minded
4. Love of learning – seeing ignorance as an opportunity
5. Perspective – putting ourselves in the shoes of others and weighing up good advice

Courage

Courage often requires the will to look at things realistically and at the same time to have a goal and to pursue it consistently.

6. Honesty – daring to be honest
7. Bravery – confronting challenges
8. Perseverance – persisting through rough patches
9. Zest – daring to be enthusiastic

Humanity

Humanity often manifests itself in love for other people and in prioritizing love for people

10. Love – being able to allow and regulate closeness
11. Kindness – showing helpfulness and being there for others
12. Social intelligence – putting oneself in the position of the motives and feelings of others

Justice

Humans are hypersocial beings. From an evolutionary perspective, we are the only mammals that can form and move within states.

Anything that promotes community and the common good.

13. Teamwork – being able to work as a member of a team
14. Fairness – treating other people as equals
15. Leadership – taking responsibility and leadership in groups

Temperance

We can get caught up in things and become either too stubborn, too self-centered or too boisterous.

16. Forgiveness – forgiving others
17. Humility – giving others space
18. Prudence – treating things and people with care
19. Self-regulation – controlling impulses

Transcendence

People often have different ways of approaching and seeing life.

20. Appreciation of beauty and excellence – giving things and people an orderly framework
21. Gratitude – being grateful and appreciating the little things
22. Hope – thinking positively about the future despite all adversity
23. Humor – approaching life with wit, humor, joy and spontaneity
24. Spirituality – understanding yourself and your life as part of a larger order

Adapted from the VIA classification of character strengths and virtues. https://www.viacharacter.org. Original source Peterson & Seligman (2004).

Social Support

When examining casework in psychiatric or psychosocial institutions, it often becomes quickly apparent that the clients of these facilities typically have very few social contacts. Psychosocial exclusion is often pervasive, affecting material, health, and social aspects (Wampold & Imel, 2015). In assisting individuals seeking advice and patients in psychotherapy, it is crucial to consider the context, particularly the social context. Graphical representations of social participation can be helpful to get an overview of the support systems of a patient. Different social relationships can be explored such as family, friends, colleagues and social groups, and professionals in the tertiary network, such as therapists, general practitioners, social workers and nursing specialists. Network maps help depict and visualize the context, similar to the ecogram and ecomaps. When addressing the social participation of patients, it is not uncommon for psychological problems to be reflected here. This could manifest through a few individuals in a network map (e.g., few friends, few colleagues, limited family contact, possibly some contacts in professional help fields).

Often, the quality of relationships in social networks is perceived as unsupportive. Consequently, personal concerns cannot be addressed, or there are few opportunities for contact. Difficulties in social encounters and relationship development directly affect mental well-being. The interdependence of the individual and their environment is the focus of the System Person in Social Context, as well as in systemic therapy or interpersonal psychotherapy (Wampold & Imel, 2015). When clients have few social relationships and find it challenging to discuss personal issues in these relationships, their degree of isolation increases. Stressful events, difficult life situations, or experiencing stress are harder to manage. There may only be contacts in the tertiary network of professional helpers. Important questions in the exploration process are not only about what topics one can discuss with network members but also simply how often contact occurs. Some patients' closest relationship may be with their therapist, who they see every two weeks. A lack of successful social connection can be a contributing factor or trigger for mental disorders.

Searching for resources in the patient's life experiences becomes essential. By articulating resources, a patient's context becomes more visible, touching on various aspects like somatic, social, or life-world-related aspects. One can do this together with the client through the depiction of symbolically representing a collection of stones, which helps add context to the articulated resources. Such representations via stones is depicted in Figure 10, and helps elucidate the client's perception and understanding.

1) *Focus on a major topic:* A topic, a question, or burden is the starting point. Questions include: What is troubling you currently? What thoughts occupy your mind? What is your theme? What weighs down on you? The client describes to the therapist, who explores, reformulates, acknowledges, or explicates the topic. The client selects one of the stones representing the issue, burden, or question.
2) *Mapping social support:* The subsequent discussion aims to search for resources, such as friends, family, therapists, who support or help in the situation. Characteristics, valuable biographical experiences, or life-worlds that provide balance are also recognized, alongside opportunities for useful exchanges. The client places these social or personal resources on the surface. The problem is contextualized this way, becoming one stone among others, and resources are made evident. The therapist assists the client in completing the picture by exploring the significance of these resources. Depending on the relationships, questions may be like: How can you discuss the issue with this person? What do you think your friend will say? How does the person react to learning about your problem, or do they already know? What does it mean for you to discuss this issue with a trusted person? What impact could it have? When you see how this resource relates to your topic (the therapist refers to the layout), what effect does it have on you? How might it contribute to addressing your question in the future? In a dialogic process, the client envisions an image embedding their problem within their resource context, symbolized here by stones.
3) *Exploration of social support:* Personal intra-individual resources like skills, characteristics, coping experiences, or experiences of positive value are assessed, just as social resources in terms of immediate relationships and wider valuable connections like friends or family. Additionally, living conditions, like residing in a neighborhood or community with access to social or medical support, can be considered. The mere presence of certain circumstances

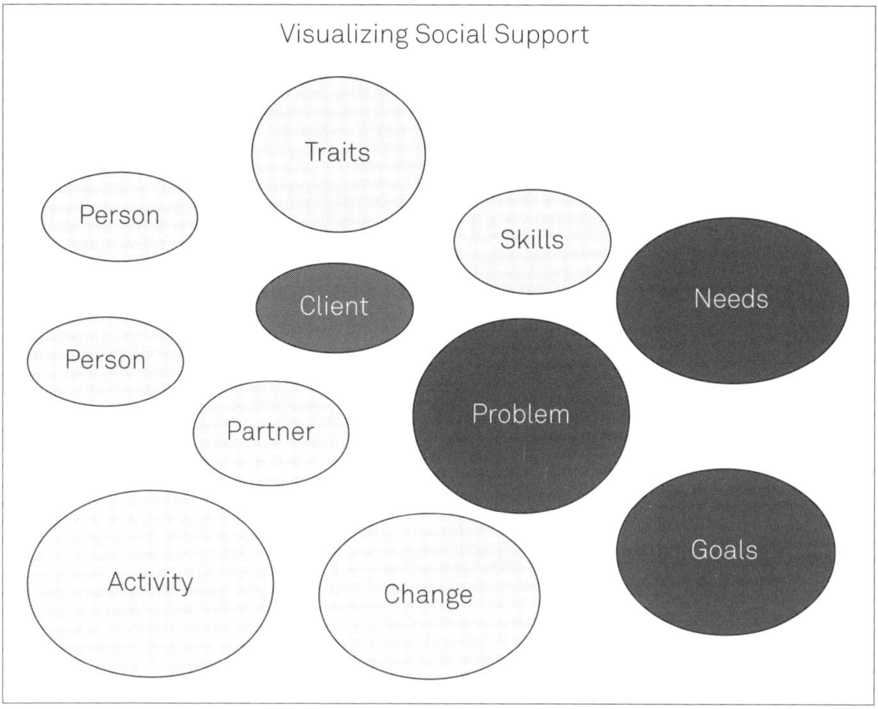

Figure 10. Visualizing the social network in symbolic representations can help to better see the redundancy of the networks. It can be crucial that a single person/an individual network is not put under too much strain and fails in the long term. Building and maintaining a sustainable overall network can take years in the case of chronic disorders.

does not constitute a resource; it is through interaction between the individual and the environment that possibilities in subjective life experiences become resources. Similar to personal resources, something becomes a resource only if the patient perceives it as one and finds it useful. In psychotherapy, and through resource articulation, these interactions between individuals and social resources can be focused on. For instance, if a patient has a good relationship with the therapist, one can attempt to transfer experienced relationship competence into daily life by guiding them towards discussing personal concerns with others, possibly drawing from previous experiences. The primary goal of resource articulation is to activate social resources.

4) *Coordination and consolidation of social support:* The articulation of resources in the context of the current problems clarifies the patient's world. This clarity not only benefits the therapist but also the patient. One can conduct an articulation of the current situation, then complement it with an

articulation of the desired situation, needs and wishes. Intermediary steps can yield actions for therapy development. A natural progression can occur when exploring the patient's concerns and subsequently situating them within the resource context. The illustration is just an example and will differ with each patient. The focus is on recognizing the extent of social support, the quality and quantity of the social network, and the scope of valuable social resources. The frequency of contacts and encounters can also be noted. The exploratory conversation can focus on identifying social and relational resources to gain insight into the client's social lifeworld. Social resources encompass the individual's social skills, attributes, and their social networks. All these social resources can be utilized to address the therapeutic mandate and goals.

Possible Difficulties

Recognized social support is generally available for working on therapy goals. Clients often increase the degree of flexibility in their own behavior in the course of therapy. These changes can both enrich and unsettle the social environment. Social support is always participatory. Therefore, make sure that the socially supportive persons are sufficiently involved in the change process (either indirectly through the client or directly in sessions).

Further Reading

Campos-Paíno, H., Moreno-Peral, P., Gómez-Gómez, I., Conejo-Cerón, S., Galán, S., Reyes-Martín, S., & Bellón, J. Á. (2022). Effectiveness of social support-based interventions in preventing depression in people without clinical depression: A systematic review and meta-analysis of randomized controlled trials. *International Journal of Social Psychiatry, 69*(2), 253–266. https://doi.org/10.1177/00207640221134232

Dealing With Uncertainties in the Therapeutic Relationship During Sessions

The working alliance proposed by Bordin emphasizes the collaborative and positive working relationship between therapist and patient. The working alliance is the most extensively researched process characteristic worldwide. Carl Rogers' humanistic approach and empirical approaches have postulated a significant influence on this pantheoretical working alliance, which is transdiagnostically and transtheoretically defined. The alliance is characterized by a mutual, collaborative, dyadic therapeutic quality between the patient and the therapist. Please see Flückiger et al., 2018 and Wampold & Flückiger, 2023, for more information about these different approaches.

The Tripartite Model

The tripartite model (Gelso, 2014) emphasizes strength-based approaches too, as an essential therapeutic relationship principle. It is essential that the therapeutic relationship is not too fast problematized but coordinated cooperatively in the sense of a joint process. A balanced understanding of patients is the key to ensuring that they feel seen in their individuality. For the majority of patients, it may quickly become apparent that the relationship feels genuine, present, and uncomplicated.

Approaching Uncertainties in the Therapeutic Relationship

Even if problematic relationship aspects of individuals are not tabooed, it should not be too hastily concluded that a patient has a problematic relationship pattern. In order to understand patients in a differentiated way, it is not enough for clinicians to be able to recognize well-described, problematic relationship patterns as quickly as possible. On the contrary, it is more important to arrive at the most balanced hypothesis possible.

The following sequence enables clinicians not to search for and find negative relationship patterns too quickly. If there is uncertainty in the therapeutic relationship during a therapy session, clinicians can ask themselves the following questions in a strength-oriented sequence (from simpler relationship uncertainties to more chronic relationship patterns):

1) *Uncertainty in the therapy agreement and working alliance?* Check whether the working alliance and the agreement on therapy tasks including therapy goals and therapy planning, are clear to both you and the patient. Are the therapeutic tasks and associated roles clear not only to you, but also to the patient? If the patient reacts immediately in a hesitant manner and you find yourself simultaneously engaging in "therapizing without a mutual therapy goal", this would be a significant indication to pause briefly and potentially take a step back in your approach.
2) *Uncertainty in the real relationship?* Check whether you are either too strongly resource-oriented in protecting the patient (e.g., "such a pity") or too strongly problematizing the patient (e.g., "such an abysmal mess"). In both extremes, there is a risk of losing sight of the productive zone of the next proximate therapeutic step. Check further whether a disturbing context influences the

relationship (e.g., patient odor, patient recalling negative situations with other persons etc.).

3) *Uncertainty in the immediate needs-oriented relationship?* Check whether you are immediately neglecting a central need or lasting motivation of a patient (see Caspar, 2024). Explore whether the conversation immediately changes when you explicitly focus on a possibly neglected need or motivational goal of the patient (e.g., giving the patient more autonomy, giving the patient more security).
4) *Uncertainty as a sign of a persistent negative relationship pattern?* Patients can test the therapy and play with the therapeutic relationship. Ruptures in the therapeutic relationship may be based on behaviors that bring the patient into therapy. The recognition of problematic patterns in the therapeutic relationship is conceptualized in practically all well-established psychotherapy orientations; e.g., in the form of interpersonal schemas, maladaptive relationship assumptions and transference patterns. If these in-session behavioral patterns are consistent across sessions, you can take some time to reflect on them. If you come to the conclusion that these relationship patterns are a hindrance to therapy, choose an appropriate form of intervention that you have thoroughly learned to directly address relationship patterns during therapy. Do not start improvising relationship experiments (Safran & Muran, 2000).

Possible Difficulties

Avoid too rapid problem-oriented relationship interpretations and try to reflect on the four questions from top to bottom. Conversely, do not avoid the questions further down if you cannot explain the uncertainty in the therapeutic relationship.

Further Reading

Caspar, F. (2024). A longitudinal view of an approach to responsiveness: Principles followed and lessons learned. *Psychotherapy Research, 34*(8), 1019–1034. https://doi.org/10.1080/10503307.2023.2275627

Eubanks, C. F., Samstag, L. W., & Muran, J. C. (2022). *Rupture and repair in psychotherapy: A critical process for change.* American Psychological Association. https://doi.org/10.1037/0000306-000

Gelso, C. (2013). A tripartite model of the therapeutic relationship: Theory, research, and practice. *Psychotherapy Research, 24*(2), 117–131. https://doi.org/10.1080/10503307.2013.845920

Flückiger, C., Del Re, A. C., Wampold, B. E., & Horvath, A. O. (2018). The alliance in adult psychotherapy: A meta-analytic synthesis. *Psychotherapy, 55*(4), 316–340. https://doi.org/10.1037/pst0000172

4 Empirical Evidence of Assessing and Working With Patient Strength

Based on an interdisciplinary task force initiated by Hill and Norcross (2023) to investigate basic psychotherapy skills and methods Flückiger et al. (2023) systematized the empirical evidence of strength-based methods as an umbrella term for psychotherapy augmentation strategies that systematize on patients' strengths. Their systematic review was twofold: It aimed to assess in-session strength-based methods under bona fide psychotherapy settings and their link to intermediate outcomes, and to conduct a comparative meta-analysis of trials examining strength-based psychotherapies against other bona fide psychotherapies. Inclusion criteria mandated that studies referring to interventions as "strength-based," "solution-focused," "resource-oriented," or "resilience-based," involve patients with a current mental health diagnosis, entail bona fide psychotherapy, and ensure comparable treatment conditions. Excluded were studies focusing on children, couples, or family therapy, preventive programs, or pilot studies with fewer than 10 participants or less than three therapists. For bona fide psychotherapy classification, studies had to involve treatments recognized as legitimate (e.g., CBT, psychodynamic therapy), a description referencing a psychological mechanism, use of a treatment manual or guide, and incorporation of an active component based on psychological literature.

Prior Meta-Analyses

Prior meta-analyses indicate a broad range of treatment outcomes in favor of strength-based methods particularly due to the variety of investigated control groups, subclinical populations, and targeted problems (see Table 4). Overall, the results mostly indicate small effects in favor of strength-based methods. For practitioners, the most relevant question probably is whether the existing legitimate (bona fide) psychotherapies can be enhanced by adjunct strength-based methods.

Table 4. Prior meta-analytic summaries

Authors	k	*N*	Targeted mental health suffering	Comparison	Outcomes	Posttreatment outcomes
Bolier et al., 2013	39	6139	Psychosocial problems	NI, WL, TAU, PL	WB, DS	Increase of positive outcomes: + Decrease of symptoms: +
Chakhssi et al., 2018	30	1864	Mental and somatic disorders	AC, NI, WL	WB, DS	Increase of positive outcomes: + Decrease of symptoms: 0
Munder et al., 2019	10	918	Mental disorders	WL, AC	PS, IF, QoL	Decrease of symptoms: +
Sin & Lyubomirsky, 2009	51	4266	DS	NT, PL, TAU, NC	WB, DS	Increase of positive outcomes: + Decrease of symptoms: +
White et al., 2019	51/ 39	4266/ 6139	DS, psychosocial problems	NT, WL, TAU, PL	WB, DS	Increase of positive outcomes: +/0 Decrease of symptoms: r = +
Hoppen & Morina, 2021	20	1360	Mental and somatic disorders	WL, AC	WB, Symptoms	Increase of positive outcomes: ++ Decrease of symptoms: ++
Flückiger et al., 2023	9	804	Mental disorders	Bona fide, legitimate psychotherapy	Symptoms	Decrease of symptoms: +

Note. k = number of studies included; *N* = patient sample size; AC = active control group; PL = placebo; NI = no intervention; NT= no treatment; NC = neutral control group; TAU = treatment as usual; WL = waitlist. Outcomes: WB = well-being; DS = depressive symptoms; BMI = body-mass index; PS = primary symptoms; IF = interpersonal functioning; QoL = quality of life; *d* = Cohen's d; *g* = Hedges' g; Z_r = mean Fisher effect size; + = small effects in favor of strength-based methods (SBM), ++ = strong effects in favor of SBM, 0 = not significant (positive) effects . Adapted from Flückiger et al., 2023.

Search Strategy for Bona Fide Comparisons

The systematic search spanned multiple databases including PsycINFO, ERIC, MEDLINE, and PSYNDEX, integrating keywords linked to strength-based psychotherapies and clinical trials. We reviewed prior meta-analyses and examined introductions and references of included studies to find relevant process-outcome studies. Additionally, a separate search was conducted using terms specific to resource activation. From 2,887 unique articles, 8 process-outcome studies and 9 comparative trials were identified. Agreement on study inclusion was high among raters, and coding discrepancies were resolved by consensus.

Process-Outcome Studies – Review

The review of eight process-outcome studies revealed consistent positive associations between strength-based methods and session-level outcomes. The studies demonstrated that when therapists integrated strength-based methods into sessions, it often correlated with favorable patient assessments of session productivity and engagement, even when initial patient response was inadequate. Strength-based methods appeared particularly effective in enhancing patients' perception of session productivity when therapist interventions were tailored to individual skills and strengths.

Comparative Meta-Analysis

The meta-analysis employed a multi-level random-effects model to account for multiple outcomes per study, examining variance within and between studies (see Table 5). The 57 effect sizes from 9 trials indicated a modest but significant advantage (g = 0.166) for strengths-based psychotherapies compared to other bona fide psychotherapies. This finding supports the potential utility of strength-based methods as psychotherapy augmentation strategies. Note that the majority of included outpatients suffered from anxiety and/or depression.

Effect on Disorder-Specific Outcomes

A moderator analysis considered disorder-specific outcomes as potential moderators, hypothesizing that measures specific to certain disorders might yield different effect sizes than those assessing well-being. Results showed that targeted disorder-specific outcomes did demonstrate marginally higher effect sizes in strength-based methods than broacher outcomes, suggesting a nuanced understanding of effectiveness based on targeted therapeutic populations.

The systematic review and meta-analysis underline the potential of strength-based methods for sustainable psychotherapy outcomes. The findings support the utility of strength-based methods in clinical settings, advocating for their integration as augmentation strategies in established psychotherapeutic practices. It should be noted that established psychotherapeutic practices already focus to some extent on patients' strengths. The evidence supports the continued investigation into strength-based methods, emphasizing their context-dependent adaptability and potential to foster more favorable therapy outcomes. Overall, the comprehensive analysis provides robust support for incorporating strength-based methods into psychotherapy, advocating for further exploration of their specific mechanisms and broader implementation in clinical practice to optimize therapeutic efficacy. The potential utility of strength-based methods on treatment outcomes was attributed as "demonstrably effective" by the above-mentioned intersectional APA-Task force (Hill & Norcross, 2023).

Our systematic review of strength-based approaches in therapy sessions, along with a meta-analysis of comparative trials, suggests that strength-based methods can enhance the effectiveness of psychotherapy. The meta-analytic evidence shows that adjunct, strength-based psychotherapies are as effective as, and sometimes slightly more effective than other legitimate psychotherapies. Based on this research evidence, we recommend that practitioners:

- Consider incorporating strength-based methods throughout all phases of treatment.
- Include the assessment of strengths during the clinical interview and standardized assessments, explicitly discussing both weaknesses and strengths with the patient.
- Integrate both weaknesses and strengths into case formulation to achieve a more balanced and comprehensive understanding of the patient's narrative and needs.
- Be aware that assessing positive constructs may reveal problematic aspects of functioning (e.g., low self-esteem, hope, gratitude, kindness).

Table 5. Comparative trials contrasting legitimate psychotherapy with augmented strengths-based methods vs. legitimate (bona fide) psychotherapy

Study	Patient population	Depression or anxiety comorbidities excluded	SUD excluded	Strengths-based condition	Bona fide comparison	*N*	Effect size
Boyer et al., 2015	ADHD	yes	yes	Solution-focused therapy + Motivational interviewing	Manualized CBT (Plan My Life) + Motivational Interviewing	159	=
Cheavens et al., 2012	Major depression	no	yes	Modular CBT for depression: Two treatment modules were selected to reflect individual patients' strengths	Modular: Two treatment modules were selected to reflect individual patients' deficits	42	++
Flückiger & Holtforth, 2008	multidiagnostic (depression & anxiety)	no	yes	Custom tailored CBT: Manualized CBT: (a) Case formulation of patients' strengths, (b) tailoring CBT to match patients' strengths	Custom tailored CBT: (a) Case formulation without augmented focus on patients' strengths, (b) use of CBT as usual	40	++
Flückiger et al., 2016	GAD	no	no	Manualized CBT: (a) Case formulation of patients' strengths, (b) tailoring CBT to match patients' strengths	Manualized CBT: (a) Case formulation of patients' symptoms, (b) tailoring CBT to match patients' symptoms	57	+

Table 5. Continued

Study	Patient population	Depression or anxiety comorbidities excluded	SUD excluded	Strengths-based condition	Bona fide comparison	*N*	Effect size
Flückiger et al., 2021	GAD	no	no	Manualized CBT: (a) Case formulation of patients' strengths, (b) tailoring CBT to patient's change behaviors	Manualized CBT: (a) Case formulation of patients' symptoms, (b) tailoring CBT to match patients' symptoms	80	+
Knekt et al., 2008	multidiag-nostic (depression & anxiety)	no	yes	Solution-focused therapy	Short-term psychody-namic therapy	198	=
Kosfelder, 2000	Anxiety disorder	no	yes	Custom tailored CBT: CBT + Solution-focused methods (focus on previ-ous solution attempts, early change, compli-ments)	Custom tailored CBT: CBT as usual	75	=
Teismann et al., 2011	Major depression	no	yes	Manualized CBT: (a) So-lution-focused methods (focus on previous solu-tion at tempts, early change, compliments),	Manualized CBT: CBT as usual	70	=

Table 5. Continued

Study	Patient population	Depression or anxiety comorbidities excluded	SUD excluded	Strengths-based condition	Bona fide comparison	*N*	Effect size
				(b) strengths-oriented modification of CBT techniques (e.g., finding functional cognitions without elaborating dysfunctional cognitions)			
Willutzki et al , 2004	SAD	yes	yes	Manualized CBT: (a) Solution-focused methods (focus on previous solution attempts, early change, compliments), (b) strengths-oriented modification of CBT techniques (finding functional cognitions without elaborating dysfunctional cognitions)	Manualized CBT: CBT as usual	83	**

Note. ADHD = attention deficit hyperactivity disorder, GAD = generalized anxiety disorder, SAD = social anxiety disorder, SUD = substance use disorder, CBT = cognitive behavioral therapy, effect sizes at posttreatment in favor of strength-based methods: = nonsignificant effects, + small effects, ++ considerable effects. Adapted from Flückiger et al., 2023.

- Collaborate with patients to define and amplify their strengths. Therapists and patients might have differing opinions on the value or meaning of certain strengths and in the patient's functioning. A culturally sensitive approach is crucial in these cases.
- Consider obtaining an external perspective from someone significant in the patient's life regarding the patient's strengths; this can sometimes provide beneficial information, which the patient is unaware of.
- Use strength-based methods to enhance and broaden the success of therapy in terms of the World Health Organization (WHO)'s definition of mental health (e.g., symptom reduction, well-being, psychosocial participation) (WHO, 2025).
- Develop language or expressions that convey inclusiveness and positive regard (e.g., "You just mentioned a highlight moment. What does that mean to you?", "This voice representing your inner critic, does it have something wise to share, or is it simply critical?").
- Monitor and validate positive changes across all aspects of psychosocial functioning throughout the therapy.
- Identify and discuss with the patient the functional aspects of behaviors that might be easily dismissed as dysfunctional (by either the therapist or the patient).
- Recognize existing problem-solving strategies to facilitate behavioral change and use these strategies to develop new skills.
- Incorporate patient strengths into homework assignments (e.g., noting positive moments or experiences during a week, planning enjoyable activities) and in encouraging activities outside the therapy room (e.g., recreation, physical exercise, social support).
- Be cautious that emphasizing strengths may not always align with the patient's experience. For instance, a therapist overwhelmed by the patient's despair might attempt to *cheer them up* and *focus on the positive*. This approach could lead the patient to feel invalidated and isolated if their distress is not appropriately addressed.
- There is something very natural and human about the use of strength-based methods. What matters is not the very specific intervention, but the more general attitude and focus of attention to integrate strength-based methods into legitimate psychotherapies.
- Strength-based methods are often simply (or not so simply) forgotten in everyday clinical practice.

Further Reading

Hill, C. E., & Norcross, J. C. (2023). Skills and methods that work in psychotherapy: Observations and conclusions from the special issue. *Psychotherapy, 60*(3), 407–416. https://doi.org/10.1037/pst0000487

Flückiger, C., Munder, T., Del Re, A. C., & Solomonov, N. (2023). Strength-based methods – a narrative review and comparative multilevel meta-analysis of positive interventions in clinical settings. *Psychotherapy Research, 33*(7), 856–872. https://doi.org/10.1080/10503307.2023.2181718

References

Bagheri, M., Woud, M. L., Simon, J., Abdalla, L., Dombrowe, M., Woinek, C., Margraf, J., & Blackwell, S. E. (2024). Inducing positive involuntary mental imagery in daily life using personalized photograph stimuli. *Memory, 33*(1), 31–44. https://doi.org/10.1080/09658211.2024.2402920

Bandura, A. (1986). *Social foundations of thought and action: Social cognitive theory.* Prentice-Hall, Inc.

Baumeister, R. F. (2005). *The cultural animal.* Oxford University Press. https://doi.org/10.1093/acprof:oso/9780195167030.001.0001

Boehnke, J. R., & Croudace, T. J. (2016). Calibrating well-being, quality of life and common mental disorder items: Psychometric epidemiology in public mental health research. *The British Journal of Psychiatry: The Journal of Mental Science, 209*(2), 162–168. https://doi.org/10.1192/bjp.bp.115.165530

Bolier, L., Haverman, M., Westerhof, G. J., Riper, H., Smit, F., & Bohlmeijer, E. T. (2013). Positive psychology interventions: A meta-analysis of randomized controlled studies. *BMC Public Health, 13*(1), Article 119. https://doi.org/10.1186/1471-2458-13-119

Boyer, B. E., Geurts, H. M., Prins, P. J., & Van der Oord, S. (2015). Two novel CBTs for adolescents with ADHD: The value of planning skills. *European Child & Adolescent Psychiatry, 24*(9), 1075–1090. https://doi.org/10.1007/s00787-014-0661-5

Broda, M. D., Granger, K., Chow, J., & Ross, E. (2023). Using social network analysis in applied psychological research: A tutorial. *Psychological Methods, 28*(4), 791–805. https://doi.org/10.1037/met0000451

Caspar, F. (2024). A longitudinal view of an approach to responsiveness: Principles followed and lessons learned. *Psychotherapy Research, 34*(8), 1019–1034. https://doi.org/10.1080/10503307.2023.2275627

Chakhssi, F., Kraiss, J. T., Sommers-Spijkerman, M., & Bohlmeijer, E. T. (2018). The effect of positive psychology interventions on well-being and distress in clinical samples with psychiatric or somatic disorders: A systematic review and meta-analysis. *BMC Psychiatry, 18*(1), Article 211. https://doi.org/10.1186/s12888-018-1739-2

Cheavens, J. S., Strunk, D. R., Lazarus, S. A. & Goldstein, L. A. (2012). The compensation and capitalization models: A test of two approaches to individualizing the treatment of depression. *Behaviour Research and Therapy, 50*(11), 699–706. https://doi.org/10.1016/j.brat.2012.08.002

Cole, M., John-Steiner, V., Scribner, S. & Souberman, E. (Eds.). (1978). *L. S. Vygotsky – Mind in society: The development of higher processes.* Harvard UP.

De Shazer, S. (1988). *Clues. Investigating solutions in brief therapy.* Norton.

Duckworth, A. L., Steen, T. A., & Seligman, M. E. (2004). Positive psychology in clinical practice. *Annual Review of Clinical Psychology, 1*(1), 629–651. https://doi.org/10.1146/annurev.clinpsy.1.102803.144154

Falconier, M. K., Jackson, J. B., Hilpert, P., & Bodenmann, G. (2015). Dyadic coping and relationship satisfaction: A meta-analysis. *Clinical Psychology Review, 42*, 28–46. https://doi.org/10.1016/j.cpr.2015.07.002

Flückiger, C., Caspar, F., Holtforth, M. G., & Willutzki, U. (2009). Working with patients' strengths: A microprocess approach. *Psychotherapy Research, 19*(2), 213–223. https://doi.org/10.1080/10503300902755300

Flückiger, C., Del Re, A. C., Wampold, B. E., & Horvath, A. O. (2018). The alliance in adult psychotherapy: A meta-analytic synthesis. *Psychotherapy, 55*(4), 316–340. https://doi.org/10.1037/pst0000172

Flückiger, C., Forrer, L., Schnider, B., Bättig, I., Bodenmann, G., & Zinbarg, R. E. (2016). A single-blinded, randomized clinical trial of how to implement an evidence-based treatment for generalized anxiety disorder [IMPLEMENT] – effects of three different strategies of implementation. *EBioMedicine, 3*, 163–171. https://doi.org/10.1016/j.ebiom.2015.11.049

Flückiger, C., & Holtforth, M. G. (2008). Focusing the therapist's attention on the patient's strengths: A preliminary study to foster a mechanism of change in outpatient psychotherapy. *Journal of Clinical Psychology, 64*(7), 876–890. https://doi.org/10.1002/jclp.20493

Flückiger, C., Kolle, C., Schürmann-Vengels, J., Rummer, R., & Allemand, M. (2025). Are psychotherapists' first clinical impressions fundamentally biased? An experimental approach. *Journal of Counseling Psychology, 72*(1), 45–55. https://doi.org/10.1037/cou0000766

Flückiger, C., Munder, T., Del Re, A. C., & Solomonov, N. (2023). Strength-based methods – a narrative review and comparative multilevel meta-analysis of positive interventions in clinical settings. *Psychotherapy Research, 33*(7), 856–872. https://doi.org/10.1080/10503307.2023.2181718

Flückiger, C., Vîslă, A., Wolfer, C., Hilpert, P., Zinbarg, R. E., Lutz, W., Holtforth, M. G., & Allemand, M. (2021). Exploring change in cognitive-behavioral therapy for generalized anxiety disorder – a two-arms ABAB crossed-therapist randomized clinical implementation trial. *Journal of Consulting and Clinical Psychology, 89*(5), 454–468. https://doi.org/10.1037/ccp0000639

Flückiger, C., Zinbarg, R. E., Znoj, H., & Ackert, M. (2013). Resource activation in generalized anxiety – an observer-based microprocess analysis of patients' in-session outcomes. *Psychotherapy, 51*(4), 535–545. https://doi.org/10.1037/a0034119

Gelso, C. (2014). A tripartite model of the therapeutic relationship: Theory, research, and practice. *Psychotherapy Research, 24*(2), 117–131. https://doi.org/10.1080/10503307.2013.845920

Grawe, K. (2004). *Psychological therapy*. Hogrefe.

Grawe, K. (2006). *Neuropsychotherapy*. Erlbaum.

Hartman, A. (1995). Dynamic assessment of family relationships. *Families in Society, 76*(2), 111–122. https://doi.org/10.1177/104438949507600207

Heckhausen, J. & Heckhausen, H. (2010). *Motivation and action*. Cambridge University Press.

Hill, C. E., & Norcross, J. C. (2023). Skills and methods that work in psychotherapy: Observations and conclusions from the special issue. *Psychotherapy, 60*(3), 407–416. https://doi.org/10.1037/pst0000487

Hoppen, T. H., & Morina, N. (2021). Efficacy of positive psychotherapy in reducing negative and enhancing positive psychological outcomes: A meta-analysis of randomised controlled trials. *BMJ Open, 11*(9), Article e046017. https://doi.org/10.1136/bmjopen-2020-046017

Howard, K. I., Lueger, R. J., Maling, M. S., & Martinovich, Z. (1993). A phase model of psychotherapy outcome: Causal mediation of change. *Journal of Consulting and Clinical Psychology, 61*(4), 678–685. https://doi.org/10.1037/0022-006x.61.4.678

Knekt, P., Lindfors, O., Härkänen, T., Välikoski, M., Virtala, E., Laaksonen, M. A., Marttunen, M., Kaipainen, M., Renlund, C., & Helsinki Psychotherapy Study Group. (2008). Randomized trial on the effectiveness of long-and short-term psychodynamic psychotherapy and solution-focused therapy on psychiatric symptoms during a 3-year follow-up. *Psychological Medicine, 38*(5), 689–703. https://doi.org/10.1017/S003329170700164X

Kosfelder, J. (2000). *Handlungsorientierung durch Lösungsfokus. Eine klinisch-psychologische Interventionsstudie* [Action orientation through solution focus. A clinical psychological intervention study]. Der Andere Verlag.

Krebs, P., Norcross, J. C., Nicholson, J. M., & Prochaska, J. O. (2018). Stages of change and psychotherapy outcomes: A review and meta-analysis. *Journal of Clinical Psychology, 74*(11), 1964–1979. https://doi.org/10.1002/jclp.22683

McGoldrick, M., Gerson, R., & Petry, S. (2020). *Genograms: Assessment and treatment.* Norton.

Moggia, D., Lutz, W., Arndt, A., & Feixas, G. (2020). Patterns of change and their relationship to outcome and follow-up in group and individual psychotherapy for depression. *Journal of Consulting and Clinical Psychology, 88*(8), 757–773. https://doi.org/10.1037/ccp0000562

Munder, T., Karcher, A., Yadikar, Ö., Szeles, T., & Gumz, A. (2019). Focusing on patients' existing resources and strengths in cognitive-behavioral therapy and psychodynamic therapy: A systematic review and meta-analysis. *Zeitschrift für Psychosomatische Medizin und Psychotherapie, 65*(2), 144–161. https://doi.org/10.13109/zptm.2019.65.2.144

Niemiec, R. M. (2018). *Character strengths interventions.* Hogrefe.

Norman, G. R., & Eva, K. W. (2010). Diagnostic error and clinical reasoning. *Medical Education, 44*(1), 94–100. https://doi.org/10.1111/j.1365-2923.2009.03507.x

Peterson, C., & Seligman, M. E. P. (2004). *Character strengths and virtues: A handbook and classification.* Oxford University Press, American Psychological Association.

Rashid, T. (2009). Positive interventions in clinical practice. *Journal of Clinical Psychology, 65*(5), 461–466. https://doi.org/10.1002/jclp.20588

Safran, J. D. & Muran, J. C. (2000). *Negotiating the therapeutic alliance: A relational treatment guide.* Guilford Press.

Scheel, M. J., Davis, C. K., & Henderson, J. D. (2012). Therapist use of client strengths. *The Counseling Psychologist, 41*(3), 392–427. https://doi.org/10.1177/0011000012439427

Shalom, J. G., & Aderka, I. M. (2020). A meta-analysis of sudden gains in psychotherapy: Outcome and moderators. *Clinical Psychology Review, 76*, Article 101827. https://doi.org/10.1016/j.cpr.2020.101827

Sin, N. L., & Lyubomirsky, S. (2009). Enhancing well-being and alleviating depressive symptoms with positive psychology interventions: A practice-friendly meta-analysis. *Journal of Clinical Psychology, 65*(5), 467–487. https://doi.org/10.1002/jclp.20593

Smith, E. C., & Grawe, K. (2003). What makes psychotherapy sessions productive? A new approach to bridging the gap between process research and practice. *Clinical Psychology & Psychotherapy, 10*(5), 275–285. https://doi.org/10.1002/cpp.377

Smith, E. C., & Grawe, K. (2005). Which therapeutic mechanisms work when? A step towards the formulation of empirically validated guidelines for therapists' session-to-session decisions. *Clinical Psychology & Psychotherapy, 12*(2), 112–123. https://doi.org/10.1002/cpp.427

Teismann, T., Dymel, W., Schulte, D., & Willutzki, U. (2011). Ressourcenorientierte Akutbehandlung unipolarer Depressionen: Eine randomisierte kontrollierte Psychotherapiestudie [Resource-oriented acute treatment of unipolar depression: A randomized controlled psychotherapy study]. *Psychotherapie, Psychosomatik und Medizinische Psychologie, 61*(7), 295–302. https://doi.org/10.1055/s-0030-1270453

Wampold, B. E., & Flückiger, C. (2023). The alliance in mental health care: Conceptualization, evidence and clinical applications. *World Psychiatry, 22*(1), 25–41. https://doi.org/10.1002/wps.21035

Wampold, B. E., & Imel, Z. E. (2015). *The great psychotherapy debate: The evidence for what makes psychotherapy work* (2nd ed.). Routledge/Taylor & Francis Group.

White, C. A., Uttl, B., & Holder, M. D. (2019). Meta-analyses of positive psychology interventions: The effects are much smaller than previously reported. *PLoS ONE, 14*(5), Article e0216588. https://doi.org/10.1371/journal.pone.0216588

WHO (2025). *Mental health.* https://www.who.int/news-room/fact-sheets/detail/mental-health-strengthening-our-response

Willutzki, U., Haas, H., Neumann, B., Koban, C., & Schulte, D. (2004). Zur Psychotherapie sozialer Ängste: Kognitive Verhaltenstherapie im Vergleich zu einem kombiniert ressourcenorientierten Vorgehen. Eine randomisierte kontrollierte Interventionsstudie [Psychotherapy for social anxiety: Cognitive behavioral therapy compared to a combined resource-oriented approach. A randomized controlled intervention study]. *Zeitschrift für Klinische Psychologie und Psychotherapie, 33*(1), 42–50. https://doi.org/10.1026/0084-5345.33.1.42

Appendix

The following materials for your book can be downloaded free of charge once you register on the Hogrefe website.

Handout 1. Resource Priming
Handout 2. Resource-Oriented Dialogue Strategies – Possible Questions
Handout 3. Differentiating Positive Feelings and Moods
Handout 4. Exploring Change
Handout 5. List of 24 Character Strengths

How to proceed:

DOWNLOAD

1. Go to www.hgf.io/media and create a user account. If you already have one, please log in.

2. Go to **My supplementary materials** in your account dashboard and enter the code below. You will automatically be redirected to the download area, where you can access and download the supplementary materials.

   Code: B-Q1XVD5

To make sure you have permanent direct access to all the materials, we recommend that you download them and save them on your computer.

Handout 1

Resource Priming

	Resource hotspots		How can they be activated?		How strongly was the resource activated?				
	Test battery/clinical impression	Importance	Within therapy	Outside of therapy	Session 1	Session 2	Session 3	Session 4	Session 5
1									
2									
3									
4									
5									
Further resources over the course of the therapy									

How strongly was the resource activated? 4 = extremely; 3 = very; 2 = fairly; 1 = somewhat; 0 = not at all.

This is a **preview** of the content that is available in the downloadable material of this book. Please see p. 81 for instructions on how to obtain the full-sized, printable PDF.

Handout 2

Resource-Oriented Strategies – Possible Questions

1) Perceiving and validating directly available resources
   - Have I honored the unproblematic results of a questionnaire?
   - Have I properly strengthened behavior that is useful to the therapy?
   - What difference does the patient's coming to therapy make?

vs. Actively introducing unused resources
   - Does the patient have skills that were forgotten in the actual situation?
   - Does the patient have skills he or she does not dare to use yet?
   - Is a step in the right direction being made?

2) Verbalizing resources
   - Can I picture the resource the patient is describing to me?
   - Have I understood the subjective significance of the resource for the person?
   - What does the person's "beaming" mean when they tell a story?

vs. Making resources immediately experienceable
   - What brings joy to the patient and can I integrate this into the process?
   - How can I adapt the therapy process to suit the patient's skills?
   - Do I adapt the therapy process to the patient's "environment" (language, metaphors, nonverbal cues)?

3) Strengthening personal resources
   - What is the patient passionate about?
   - What does the person feel committed to?
   - What leaves the patient cold? And why?

vs. Boosting the resources of the social network
   - Are there strong role models in their family or circle of friends?
   - In what areas can the patient count on social support?
   - Is there someone the patient trusts?

4) Picking up existing or unused skills and talents (potential resources)
   - What is the person particularly good at?
   - What comes natural to them?
   - When does the person begin to "flow"?

vs. Integrating existing goals and desires (motivational resources)
   - What dreams does the patient nurture?
   - What idols does the person have?
   - In what areas does the person have positive expectations of change?

5) Focusing on problem-independent resources
   - In what areas does the patient perceive themselves as being competent?
   - Were there good times in the past?
   - Did I make time to allow the patient to rave about their passions?

vs. Taking advantage of problem-relevant resources
   - To what extent can the problem be defined?
   - Are there exceptions?
   - What is the effect of the improvements that have occurred?
   - To what extent can I validate the understanding of the problem?

6) Optimizing usable resources
   - To what extent can a resource be exhausted?
   - What are the limits of a usable resource?
   - What is means-ends relationship?

vs. Maintaining trainable resources
   - Have I repeated the results enough?
   - Is regularity useful?
   - Is there any potential for variation?

This is a **preview** of the content that is available in the downloadable material of this book. Please see p. 81 for instructions on how to obtain the full-sized, printable PDF.

Handout 3

Differentiating Positive Feelings and Moods

Feeling/mood	Magnitude	Situation
Cheerful, happy		
Untroubled		
Excited, euphoric		
Relaxed, calm		
Longing, enraptured		
Optimistic		
Proud		
Active		
Alert		
Interested		
Decisive		

Magnitude: 1 = slightly; 2 = noticeable; 3 = pronounced; 4 = strong; 5 = maximum level.

This is a **preview** of the content that is available in the downloadable material of this book. Please see p. 81 for instructions on how to obtain the full-sized, printable PDF.

Handout 4

Exploring Change

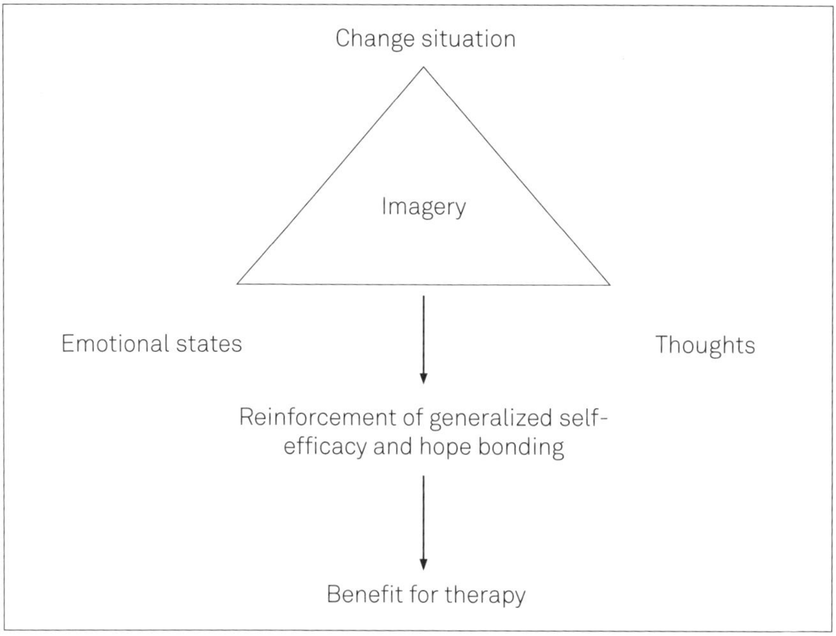

This is a **preview** of the content that is available in the downloadable material of this book.
Please see p. 81 for instructions on how to obtain the full-sized, printable PDF.

Handout 5

List of 24 Character Strengths

Wisdom

Wisdom goes beyond lexical knowledge and relates to a person's entire life experience.
1. Creativity – finding new solutions
2. Curiosity – being interested
3. Judgment – weighing things up carefully; being open-minded
4. Love of learning – seeing ignorance as an opportunity
5. Perspective – putting ourselves in the shoes of others and weighing up good advice

Courage

Courage often requires the will to look at things realistically and at the same time to have a goal and to pursue it consistently.
6. Honesty – daring to be honest
7. Bravery – confronting challenges
8. Perseverance – persisting through rough patches
9. Zest – daring to be enthusiastic

Humanity

Humanity often manifests itself in love for other people and in prioritizing love for people
10. Love – being able to allow and regulate closeness
11. Kindness – showing helpfulness and being there for others
12. Social intelligence – putting oneself in the position of the motives and feelings of others

Justice

Humans are hypersocial beings. From an evolutionary perspective, we are the only mammals that can form and move within states.
Anything that promotes community and the common good.
13. Teamwork – being able to work as a member of a team
14. Fairness – treat other people as equals
15. Leadership – taking responsibility and leadership in groups

Temperance

We can get caught up in things and become either too stubborn, too self-centered or too boisterous.
16. Forgiveness – forgiving others
17. Humility – giving others space
18. Prudence – treating things and people with care
19. Self-regulation – controlling impulses

Transcendence

People often have different ways of approaching and seeing life.
20. Appreciation of beauty and excellence – giving things and people an orderly framework
21. Gratitude – being grateful and appreciating the little things
22. Hope – thinking positively about the future despite all adversity
23. Humor – approaching life with wit, humor, joy and spontaneity
24. Spirituality – understanding yourself and your life as part of a larger order

This is a **preview** of the content that is available in the downloadable material of this book. Please see p. 81 for instructions on how to obtain the full-sized, printable PDF.

Peer Commentaries

This book has the potential to fundamentally transform the practice of psychotherapy worldwide. It offers a clear, practice-oriented clinical guide demonstrating how systematic resource activation can enhance the effectiveness of existing psychotherapeutic approaches. From a structured framework for assessing patient resources alongside difficulties, through concrete dialogical strategies, to a rich repertoire of resource-activating interventions, the authors provide clinicians with actionable tools grounded in empirical research. Written by leading figures in psychotherapy theory, research, and practice, this volume is an invaluable resource for clinicians who seek to see the person beyond pathology and to foster change by building on patients' existing capacities and prior successes.

Sigal Zilcha-Mano, PhD, Professor of Clinical Psychology, Department of Psychology, University of Haifa, Israel

Filled with practical and actionable suggestions, Resource Activation in Psychotherapy *is a valuable counterweight to the mental health field's focus on pathology and problems. The authors draw on their deep knowledge of the empirical research as well as wisdom clearly borne out of clinical experience to make a compelling case for the value of collaborating with clients to recognize and capitalize on their strengths.*

Catherine F. Eubanks, PhD, Gordon F. Derner School of Psychology, Adelphi University, Garden City, NY, USA

This is an inspiring call for the mental health field to broaden its perspective; from a focus on deficits and symptom remediation toward a focus on strengths and life enhancement. Scientifically compelling, yet practical and didactic, this book belongs in the top shelf of the effective therapist's toolkit.

Jaime Delgadillo, PhD, Institute of Psychiatry, Psychology & Neuroscience, King's College London, UK